My Juicy ReBirth

A Journey To Healing The Feminine Through Pleasure & Sacred Process

LaTonia Taylor

LaTonia Taylor
Atlanta, Georgia

Copyright © 2019 LaTonia Taylor. All rights reserved. No part of this publication may be reproduced, stored in or introduced into a retrieval system, or transmitted, in any form or by any means (electronic, mechanical, photocopying, recording or otherwise), without the prior written permission of the copyright owner.

The scanning, uploading, and distribution of this book via the Internet or any other means without the permission of the publisher are illegal and punishable by law. Please purchase only authorized electronic editions and do not participate in or encourage electronic piracy of copyrighted materials. Your support of the author's rights is appreciated.

Limits of Liability ~ Disclaimer
Names have been changed to protect the innocent and certain identities within this story. The author and publisher shall not be liable for your misuse of this material. This book is strictly for informational purposes. The author and publisher do not guarantee that anyone following the techniques, suggestions, tips, ideas, or strategies will become successful. The author and publisher shall have neither liability nor responsibility to anyone concerning any loss or damage caused, or alleged to be caused, directly or indirectly by the information contained in this book.

Book Coach: The Self-Publishing Maven
Cover Design: Okomota
Editing: Roseann Warren, The Edit Bae
Formatting: Chris P

ISBN: 978-1-7335279-0-3

www.LaToniaTaylor.com
Printed in the United States of America

Acknowledgments

My Virgo Mother, Della who is the first Juicy Queen Mother and the original Tall Girl, that I've seen model the ownership of your sensual power without apology. It is her Ph.D. in Common Sense that advanced the wisdom that comes through as straight no-chaser "Mother-Wit" with my friends and clients. Most of all I am humbled by her sacrifice to ensure that I lived a comfortable life and enjoyed the deep belly laughter of learning to eavesdrop on the grown woman conversations that grounded me in womanhood.

My Sister and 2nd Mom, Shirley who is my soft place to land, straight no chaser overwhelmed my sensitive soul. While we are so very different, I give thanks that we respect and cover one another as adult women. Most of all, thank you for allowing me to co-parent your children and learn vicariously through you what "mothering" requires. Brittany may have gotten weary, but she is off to a beautiful start as a woman I adore.

All of My Grandmothers who are Ancestors who stand with me every time I allow Spirit to move through me in service to the call on my life. The greatest reward has been their nurture of my spiritual gifts. I am learning more about my bloodline, because of The Mother Code that has been activated inside of me through them. I intend to lift it.

My Tribe of Southern Mother Matriarchs whose watchful eye allowed me options for expressing the best parts of each of them. Most of all, Alice McRavin and Pinky Stewart were foundational in my relationship with Spirit and two different denominations. I'm grateful for them offering my first experience of being Spiritually bilingual.

My God-Mother, Mentor and Spiritual Covering, The Reverend Dr. Iyanla Vanzant who truly picked up where my roots left off, replanted me and supported my growth through phases from being covered in material, uncovered through self-discovery and recovered to answer the call to Ministry. I am so grateful to remember the truth of who I am with the call and response modeled by a Masterful Spiritual Technician – My Iya. My greatest honor is always to minister side by side transforming lives and continue to learn ancient alchemy of priesthoods. This work was activated by the precious, joyful moments of womanly quality time spent with my InnerVisions Mothers. I am forever grateful for "The Mamas" and my Reverend Sisters, especially Dani and Yahfaw.

My Sisters who also "mothered" me and allow me to "mother" them, even when not invited. Thank you to so many communities of women who have formed a positive circle around me as I found my orbit. There are women assigned by God to be time-tested agents of love and liberation over the years – Charise, Rashida, Cynthia, Mama Rita, Vikki, Samara, Tamara, Anika, and Journey.

My team, affectionately called Team ReBirth who started as Sister-Clients and evolved to teach me how to receive and be supported because of your embrace of Juicy in your life: Dana, Melissa, Monique, Denise, Renee, Dawn, and AraCeli your brilliance evokes Praise and Worship. Most of all I give thanks to my ALL Sister-Clients who are a treasure to my life beyond our sessions because each of you demonstrated turning a testimony into a YES-timony.

Special Thanks to My Coaches that have given me short-cuts to the lessons they have mastered.

Last and certainly not least, my Cancerian Life Partner, Shamanic Love, and husband "Baba Smokey." It was a divine set-up to partner my life under the sign of "The Nurturing Mother" as a VERY Alpha Male. You have kept my Juicy Spirit awakened and ever ready to rebirth the best parts of myself. Thank you for teaching me how to open to The Divine Masculine.

Dedication

I dedicate this book to The Mothers in my life and the process of unlocking "The Mother Code" through the Primordial Womb.

The World Is Calling Spiritually - Aligned Feminine Leaders

Are you the one?

If so read this open letter...

Dear Spiritually- Aligned Feminine Leader,

I want you to understand that you are responsible for the success or failure, improvement or stagnation, your own actions, and reactions. You are responsible for creating your visions and dreams and setting your own goals. You are responsible for believing in yourself, for improving your attitude, for developing positive habits and getting rid of the negative ones, you are responsible for your success, managing your time, seizing opportunities and controlling your emotions.

Here are a few words I want to tell you today to spark that feminine energy that carries enough magic it can change your world. Please repeat after me:

I love you today!

I honor you today!

I value my time today!

I respect you and others today!

I am growing stronger today!

I am expecting a miracle today!

I am on time today!

I am prepared today!

I am using my creativity to shine today!

I am focused today!

I am showing up in the world differently today!

Today is my day to make a difference!

It's never too late or too soon to start leading with your divine feminine energy to become a spiritually aligned successful woman. As you read this book, take each chapter, each story, and tip as permission to uplift your energy, get clear on what's next for you and make a step-by-step plan to heal YOUR life.

One of the most significant mishaps of feminine leaders is learning something that can transform your life, but never using the information you've learned to change your life. When you take action on what you've learned, you will never be the same.

As you read through this book, you will hopefully become more aware of how your feminine energy operates and will have started seeing how you have been holding yourself back from healing in numerous ways.

When the healing starts your spiritual freedom reigns.

Give up any thoughts, ideas, people, places, things, relationships that you have been hoarding. Hanging on to. Afraid to discard. Free yourself of whatever no longer serves YOU.

Make a commitment to yourself that this is the time in your life when challenges and changes are encountered. You may have been stretched in ways you did not think possible. Perhaps you have moved from crisis to crisis, and the stress seemed insurmountable.

I am here to tell you that it's all good! The Divine Feminine energy that you possess has your back, front, and sides.

Take a moment to reflect on these seven truths:

Feminine Truth #1 You are alive, ready, willing and able.

Feminine Truth #2 All that you need today is provided and tomorrow is already secured.

Feminine Truth #3 You are abundant, whole and your support team is here.

Feminine Truth #4 You are sacred--you hold the mysteries of your core feminine self.

Feminine Truth #5 You are strong, you recognize the power you possess and magic within.

Feminine Truth #6 You are beauty, wisdom, joy, peace and most importantly all things LOVE.

Feminine Truth #7 You trust in the innate abilities of your true magnificence and your brilliance.

Signed,
Your Spiritually-Aligned Feminine Sister

Lucinda Cross
Author, Speaker, Trainer
Activate Worldwide LLC.
www.lucindacross.com

Table of Contents

Our Juicy Spirit Manifesto	13
The Juicy Spirit Journey - Introduction	18
Chapter 1 : My Juicy Beginnings	27
Chapter 2 : Juicy Nudges	55
Chapter 3 : Why Juicy?	64
Chapter 4 : Pleasing God?	74
Chapter 5 : Not Juicy!	88
Chapter 6 : Pleasurably Pregnant (Juice Your Bliss)	97
Chapter 7 : Juicy Sacred Sisterhood	104
Chapter 8 : Living In The Juicy Stream?	113
Chapter 9 : The Integrated Woman	127
Closing	132
Juicy Q & A	138
About The Author	149
Juicy Programs	151

Our Juicy Spirit Manifesto

Let us begin with what we intend to manifest together, now and later when you take your juicy journey. This is a living document that continues to rebirth the lives of women who embark on the journey for the first time and those that return to its shore for another voyage.

The Juicy Journey is the integration of spiritual and sensual transformation. The Juicy Journey is activated by a woman's choice to use the messages of her life, her womb, and her unapologetic desires as a tool. Juicy Spirit is a process where women integrate the sensual, spiritual, and sweet, sacred succulence into any part of their lives that is demanding their attention. The sisterhood is a community of women holding a sacred space for women celebrating one another's unfolding on purpose, passion, and pleasure! This includes the men and partners who love them and receive benefit. Being Juicy activates a woman to hydrate herself so that her juices can flow toward the dry places in her life. Leading with Spirit is the nature of every Goddess to awaken, activate, and turn on her inner grid.

It is my heartfelt intention to invite, confirm, and provoke YOUR atonement of yourself with your higher Self, which includes your sensuality. It has never been separate. You will benefit from engaging this journey, by finding yourself and your desire to express your own womanhood in a holistic embodiment that continues to expand you and your matters of the heart. Some of you will find confirmation of what you have known, sensed or believed about your capacity to freely express sensuality without guilt or shame. However, I know for sure, that due to the low percentage of women actually experiencing regular orgasms, according to medical statistics, even more are disconnected from the relationship to their orgasmic body and their orgasmic spirit. Your story holds pieces of your mind, body, and spirit connection, therefore I share mine. As evolved as I was spiritually and metaphysically, there were matters of my womanhood that got my attention and required deeper introspection about my choices, automatic responses and unmet desires, which called me to become JUICY rather personally dehydrated by old thought forms that kept my "good-girl complex" blocking my flow.

The Juicy Spirit Woman enters a sacred space of personal communion with attention to detail and intention to accelerate her ability to seduce her potency in all matters of her life.

<u>Consider this MANIFESTO as a decree to activate your own journey to JUICY</u>. The Juicy Spirit Woman embraces that her life is a series of cycles and seasons much like a butterfly. A butterfly emerges from a cocooning process that doesn't look appealing. Therefore, to choose to enter into a process is a statement of inner power embraced with a demonstration of willingness to learn from her inner guru and transformed from merely a woman to an Alchemical Presence to her life and all those in it.

- *In personal power,* The Juicy Spirit woman accepts that she has a cape and has been Super Woman leaping over tall mountains of obstacles, met them and has overcome valley experiences that became her Superpower. She celebrates being her own shero.

- *In her desires,* The Juicy Spirit woman may manifest super feats because of her yielding to the Divine within, yet no longer needs to move through life faster than a speeding bullet, she slows down because she is willing to savor the moments of her cravings.

- *In her process of becoming,* The Juicy Spirit woman comes to her process, surrendering to the microwave results that strip her nutrition and toxify her desires at the risk of leaving traces of disappointment and spiritual amnesia. She instead chooses a slow cooker approach in the ways she notices herself, her power, her sex and sensuality.

- *In her financial affairs,* The Juicy Spirit Woman chooses herself as an act of worthiness and wealth, as a woman willing to shift legacies. She is responsible for her own Feminine Economic Development and luxury as an act of service to her contribution to the world. She embraces her business as pleasure and mixes the two every chance that she gets. This integration is her Orgasmic Abundance™.

- *In love*, The Juicy Spirit woman understands that she is no longer at war or indifferent to the loving she accepts. Instead, she is willing to risk stirring the pot of her vulnerability and authenticity in order to have her desires make room for her as she defines how she relates to her partner in a way that is co-creative, NOT codependent. She opens to conscious loving that grows and challenges her versus unconscious agreements that suck the life out of her.

- *In her bloodline*, The Juicy Spirit woman leads with forgiveness of herself first and foremost. She is no longer the sacrificial lamb of others. She interrupts patterns, even if her mother and foremothers could not or chose not to, as an act of constantly freeing herself to expand to love deeper, wider and fuller, not as a spiritual bypass. She is the healing balm to her bloodline, even if her blind spots are not hers alone.

- *In her darkness,* The Juicy Spirit woman knows her shadow and calls herself on her bullshit, when she is hiding and playing small. In fact, her Juicy self gave up her mask of pretending not to hurt. Desire, rest, and restoration and/or pain as the only thing that gets her attention.

- *In her pleasure*, The Juicy Spirit woman expands and elevates pleasure beyond poorly understood sexual power and profane and low vibe definitions by systems that do not love women. Her orgasm serves her and her vision; she invites others to partake.

- *In her elevation*, The Juicy Spirit woman elevates her pleasure, her passion, and her purpose as priceless yet worthy of her investment of time, attention, and commitment. She cannot be bought or auctioned by fear, shame, and threat, even if it's the only thing she's known.

- *In her sacredness*, The Juicy Spirit woman becomes a living scripture and her pulsating, throbbing vibration transcribes the manna of her soul into a spiritual manifestation and holy reference for women to be lifted and FREE to define their sacred relationship uniquely and unapologetically.

The Juicy Spirit Journey - Introduction

As I share with you, it is my intention to introduce to you a new language for the feminine soul or reintroduce ancient references. At other times, the words I use may have been considered profane, where they were once sacred. Indulge me. Indulge your heart, as I share my journey to juicy and observations of the rebirth of womanhood via The Juicy Journey.

I remember exploring with my best sister-friend, Charise about uniquely teaching on the spiritual aspects of pleasure and declaring the name while we were on the phone. Charise said, "Oh yes! That's you, La Tonia. That's who you are. You better reserve that name everywhere you can." I did that. Juicy Spirit sat marinating for approximately two years before I would release her as a reserved room for those ready to embark on a precious inner journey of Pleasure, Passion, and Purpose, which I call a Holy Trinity of the work of developing *"feminine pulchritude."* In simple terms, feminine beauty. The scripture is often referenced as a note of encouragement to say that *your gifts will make room for you.* While some interpret it differently amongst theologians and clergy, alike, I would have to say the unfoldment of Juicy Spirit is my living experience of this spiritual statement. I held Juicy Spirit, unbeknownst to many, as a secret group on Facebook. I added a few posts and invited only a few my inner circle. In fact, they had forgotten about it even after accepting the invitation. Isn't this true for so many matters in our life? We RSVP to private spaces inside of us and lead with an announcement to only those we trust, and then sit waiting for some magical formula to sprinkle its dust of manifestation upon us. Well, even if that does not apply to you, I can think of a few of these creative sparks lead by spirit for myself.

In the beginning, like many women, I wanted better relationships. I started to nurture the curiosity of what the Sexual, Sensual and Spiritual means through chasing orgasm. In other words, I explored the external experience and techniques for better lovemaking. Little did I know, intimacy from the secret place of womanhood would be so JUICY. Juicy and sacred opened a new level of intimacy for me and the Divine, plus all of my relationships. The Sexual, Sensual, and Spiritual to me are a Holy Atonement pattern that I uncovered during my studies and bring to the pricking process of Juicy Spirit. It is a pricking process, because Juicy Spirit is introductory, much like my own personal journey of studying sensual arts, sexual therapeutic systems, and literal techniques to grow and expand orgasmic potential. I didn't know, nor intend *any* of this when I began my study. In fact, it was quite private and like many other areas of my life, I found that my core circle of best friends had embarked on this study or was at least curious about it, as well. One of us would read or study one resource, then pass it on to the other. The others of us would attend to our personal investigation, through workshops and other practical modalities, and then pass that on. It was a self as center, investment. What I found was ancient wisdom so far beyond the benefit of expanded orgasm that required reverence and more commitment to personal healing and transformation. I devoured the obvious tantric references, commonly found in any bookstore. Each book, each conversation led me from the commercial watered-down versions of sex-centered tantra to Asian writings that told the story of mystery systems of Taoist sexual healing, secret societies that had to go underground due to politics and religious control and more. Only to find, Sexual Healing Arts had its roots in Ancient Kemet as a way of integrating the mind, body, and spirit through breath, vision or imagination and diet, mental and physical. That was a tremendous personal awakening for me.

As I continued to study Tantra, Sexual Kung Fu, Sound Healing, Touch Therapy and various forms of Yoga, I learned that sexuality is the most spiritual process of awakening the Divine within that one can devote him/herself to. To say that this is a lifestyle choice sounds far too simplistic. To me it is devotion that requires nurture and openness to see the sexuality of everything, everywhere all the time because it is creative energy that is working and transferred beyond the body. This society has reduced anything sensual and sexual to its lowest vibration and *we* have inherited it, accepted it as true and nurtured it as normal. IT IS NOT normal. The lowest vibration attracts fear of the unknown and promotes shame and guilt that recoils the most well-meaning soul away from investigating and investing in a sacred journey of the self, as Divine. On a practical level, I quickly discovered it was work to practice breath and sound techniques daily. It required conscious choices and responsibility to eat foods that generated my orgasmic life force rather than degenerated. Even my desire, to live in joy and pleasure, required reconditioning my natural propensity to trust that revelation would come through me, play with my desire and not be punished, even though I no longer believed in a hell and damnation God system. In other words, it requires discipline to feel-good and process your own life through pleasure, joy, and orgasm. I found that to simply invest in learning a technique was ego-centered and while they do work, they don't last. It's like going to school for a lifetime to get certifications and degrees, yet inside one does not truly feel validated, worthy or good enough. The road to sexual freedom is the high road, divine discourse, radical compassion, tender patience and devotion. Sacred Sensuality, Seduction, and Freedom engages your psychology, biology, and theology. So, since this is something that I was already doing as a Spiritual Psychology student and teacher, I felt activated by my discoveries. The specialty area began to choose me.

I always knew that my ministerial call was to be a bridge. I thought that it would be between those divided by religious differences. However, I found a common thread while working with women directly connected to what they believe about God, love, sex, and money had a theme. The blocks were obvious to me, yet hidden to them. I became a bridge to the religious breakdowns in women with herself and her beliefs about herself, especially her sexuality. My processes in healing and deliverance are of a sensually transformative kind. I originally thought that my ministerial call would bridge healing for leaders of congregations; instead I found a call within the call. I didn't resist this call as much as the first to ministry of spiritual consciousness. When I share with you more about my life in future works, you will hear all of the juicy details of my own rebirth and emerging transformed, over and over again.

For now, I will tell you that a common pattern in my life that I notice is the thing that I often resist, offers me a door to my own sweet unfoldment. I have found that this stubbornness is born by some long-held belief that no longer served me. Look at your patterns, as I share mine with you. So, for instance, my mother and sister always used to call me "hard-headed." Of course, I couldn't really see that if she told me something for my own good, it was at least worthy of consideration. Why? Because I held some judgments about her and her life choices on one hand and because I come from a generation of fiercely independent women, with the determination to not rely upon anyone, ask for help or admit defeat. I thought of myself as the black sheep or the ugly duckling in my family for years. Therefore, I distrusted authority (even parental) because it had not been a compassionate or generous nurturing force in my early life. I felt very criticized, rejected, and verbally abused. I was what psychologist, Elaine Aron called a Highly Sensitive Being (HSP), or an Empath, with spiritual gifts that amplified feelings that the average person will dismiss as "tough love." So, my first instinct was to reject "it" – authority. This would prove to be ironic for a natural, born leader who oftentimes resisted her own inner authority. I'm telling you, our lives speak to us if, we'd just listen. So, this message of our spirit being JUICY was a revelation that I walked with for years, like being pregnant and simply not knowing the sex or name yet. I also have the benefit of coming from a line of women who naturally embraced their sensuality and were swift with their mouths when the spirit so moved them, I played with my sexuality and seduction in the same vain. Even while covered in religious garments, my sisters and I would tickle ourselves with grown woman - no children allowed segments. It started very early in my family, though. I remember the weekends, after a hard work week, we gathered and the men would congregate outside to leave the women to "stir it up" without them. They would begin talking about the week they endured, then after run downs on the family, the neighborhood and loved ones, men and sex soon followed with the help of a few Champales, the light-weight drink of choice by my Elder crew. They didn't know were listening from the back of the house, giggling too. They each had their own sassy sensuality and I loved that about them. Now, it wasn't always positive but it was at least a conversation that I got comfortable witnessing and excited to engage in as I got older.

True to form, of resistance first, my dear Sister Minister in this field of transformation (Vikki Johnson) invited me to lead a Coaches Corner on Sensuality at her very first annual retreat. She was one of the core friends I held "sensuality" court with. I'll be honest, my initial thought was, "Of all the things she could ask me to teach, given my years of work as a spiritual teacher. THIS?" I didn't tell her that. I just embraced the fact that she wanted me to be a part of the project she was birthing. So as a Spiritual Life Coach trained by the awesome, straight, no-chaser, Reverend Dr. Iyanla Vanzant, I knew to take note of strong patterns of resistance. Therefore, I engaged my resistance with key questions. I knew there was something else going on that required my introspection. After all, I loved talking about this topic and others loved it when I did private circles and private coaching. Notice, the key word was "private," which is sometimes another code word for "hiding." I had other spiritual teachers and mentors, who are unconnected, impart the same life messages to me such as, "It's time for you to come out," "It's time to take the main stage of your life," and "You have everything that you need. Your tribe is waiting on you." My own issues of insecurity, fear, and perfectionism had delayed me so much that I couldn't see my own blind spots, even though I had been helping others to see their own. This women-centered focus on my femininity, my womb, and my sensuality was different. The impact of investigating my own resistance to go public with a sensuality focused message and process was profound. This is why it's *critical* that helping professionals are engaged in therapeutic processes themselves and have mentors that will tell hard heads the truth. I had resisted other things enough that their voices rang in my head to catch myself. I opened. I accepted. I answered the call to lead at this table.

I accepted the request to facilitate Coaches Corner on Pleasure at The Girl Talk Unplugged Getaway Retreat in April 2013. I accepted with no expectations of being more than an attendee, holding space for my sister's intimate vision, yet I had been pregnant with this program for years before receiving the request. As the date moved closer, I felt compelled to create something that would allow a woman to take on this part of her life in the safest coaching space possible. In fact, the topic area had to be revised from sensuality to pleasure with an explanation from the retreat host about what it means to the spiritual journey, just to get the attendees to feel comfortable to openly select my session. Mind you, many participants had been "churched" and afraid of judgment. Isn't that ironic? This is not because the topic was not of interest and exploration to the core audience the retreat attracted, but the shame and fear of judgment was apparent. It was a teachable moment. Needless to say, from the authentic leadership of Elder Vikki Johnson and willingness to meet this resistance head-on, my table was so full that it spilled out into the hallway and I had to turn sisters away who finally decided, "I want this!" Like me, they were resistant to stepping into their cravings. As women, we give other women permission to be fully themselves, when we set ourselves free from whatever has a hold on us. The opposite is also true with bondage because we fear the judgments of other women about our womanhood. The Universal Law of Correspondence was teaching me as I watched this moment unfold. It says, "As within, so without." The reluctant women who wanted to come to my session, were a mirror of my own reluctance when I was asked to coach this session. My sister stood for the anointing inside of me to bridge this gap for women, who through a religious mindset had become afraid of themselves and their sexuality. I am so grateful for that moment because I was healed through stepping forward and so were they. The lunchtime circle of sisters, exploring Pleasure Unplugged released and rebirthed a JUICY ministry to women, who like me had stories of religious restriction, internal conflict, broken relationships, molestation, and body image issues that acted as a plug, blocking the juices that each woman wanted to flow in her own way.

We unplugged. The moment I said, "YES" to this vision that I'd filed away was the moment, every ingredient began to unfold as a miniature rite of passage for women to introduce or reintroduce themselves to their own sensual, sexual and spiritual healing. This was the birth of Juicy Spirit.

Chapter 1: My Juicy Beginnings

"It is worse to stay where one does not belong at all than to wander about lost for a while and looking for the psychic and soulful kinship one requires." —
Clarissa Pinkola Estés

This feminine awakening journey began with my own process of self-exploration. Orgasm, Passion, and Pleasure seemed like a natural place for me to explore, since I'd spent years in other heavy-duty spiritual processes in workshops, rites of passage and leadership development from Masters in the industry of transformation, even before it was commercial. I was aware of my womanly treasures, as a result of liberating each layer of restriction. I was inspired by my big sister classmates, Dani and Yahfaw, while enrolled at The Inner Visions Institute for Spiritual Development. Our lunch breaks were lit, with the same kind of grown woman conversation that my elders had when I was a child, except we were immersed in a spiritual process. I got it as I was "coming out," then but until I gave attention to MY OWN Womb Consciousness, it was served by my "coming into" more of a deeper message from my feminine. The light touches from other women who owned their sensuality in a way that was integrated with their spiritual walk, were enough to turn a light on inside of me. That's what women do for one another, when we are free in this area of sensuality. Even today, I give thanks to my big sisters, Dani and Yahfaw for all of our lunch breaks, phone calls, and mini-sessions, while enrolled in Spiritual Life Coaching preparation at Inner Visions. They called it "Ho Training," which was an acronym for Holy One. That mentorship really helped me to embrace my womanhood on different level than my tribe mothers. While that was surely the seed, I know that I held it as a private, girls ONLY night out type of expression. Most women do. We are animated, curious and skillful storytellers in the company of our female confidants. You know it's true!

This time as a newly-wed, and alone with prayers, I heard myself praying for pregnancy. This wasn't a new prayer, though. I had desired to be a mother, years prior to being a young wife. Somehow, awareness of this unfilled desire was enough to get my attention. One morning on a 5:00 am prayer call with my sisters, I heard pray another prayer. I began speaking my prayers to my womb about my relationship with motherhood. I asked my womb to show me where it was blocked. Despite offering other forms of guidance to women helping them to formulate their vision, voice, and value, little did I know I needed this rebirth of my own womanhood. I was called to this rebirth of my relationship with "mother," "motherhood," and myself as a "mothering soul. I held a mother wound that I only addressed when I was frustrated with her. This time, I stayed present with the mother wound because I was frustrated with myself, my womb. My womb took me on a journey.

When it didn't come so easy for me the first time as a young wife, I studied the womb, herbs, and the mind/body connection, profusely. This time I was older and wiser, yet felt like my body had betrayed me, yet again. I was juicy, sexual and married, but why wasn't I getting pregnant? Answers came in various forms throughout my attempts to conceive, as each season of feeling betrayed by my womb represented a different season in my life. One theme remained.

I later learned how deeply I had unconsciously felt betrayed by authority figures in my life. I made quiet decisions about how I would do life that clearly had been absorbed into my own womb. I'll never forget the day in The Wonder Woman Weekend with Iyanla, when I asked about getting pregnant. I don't remember how I phrased it, but I'll never forget her response to me. I spoke of wanting to "give my husband a child" and she said to me, "What would it take for you to be okay with yourself, if you *never* had a child?" and that questions rocked my world. It reverberated through me from Silver Spring, Maryland, all the way to my return to Chicago, Illinois, and did not stop upon my return to do more work with her in Maryland, before I'd eventually relocate. I journaled for days and hours from *that* question and my own Inner Knowing guided me to see how I felt I *owed* my husband this child, because he had been so good to me. (Pick up your jaw!) I was shocked by my own admission to myself. I didn't stop there. I dug deeper. I began to ask myself if I thought I was worthy to be a "Kept Woman." My answers revealed to me decisions that the little girl who didn't feel safe in her own family made about my life. The answers brought me face-to-face with my inner conversations about worthiness. You see, I had never been "spoiled," although I had all that I needed. However, what I wanted seemed to come with reminders of sacrifice, frustration and struggle or an outright no. So, to have someone in my life who showered me with the lifestyle of a Queen, where I didn't have to work, jewels, luxury vehicles, backstage passes to most events, cash on demand, esteemed company, and room to grow up with the security and protection that he provided. I didn't *know* that feeling. So, my journaling from that one question from my Spiritual Mother, who I didn't know would become my Spiritual Mother, led me to a deeper truth: I thought I owed him something.

My role as a wife and a woman felt inauthentic. I began to ask myself, questions like:

1. If you felt secure about your future, would you have gotten married?
2. Why did you choose to get married?
3. Do you want the same things, now?

My answers were startling, yet freeing. All roads led me to religious conditioning and early messages about being a *good girl.*

I was in college, when I met my first husband. I didn't know who I was, yet I had become as leader in The Mosque. I'd always been a leader, in whatever I did. I felt good about myself and my relationship with God. In fact, it was the best I'd felt about "me" in a long time. Even though I had received a 4-Year Army ROTC (Reserve Officers in Training Corps) Scholarship to attend the college of my choice, the girly me had a hard time imagining my future in mud, trenches, climbing walls, running and hollering in boots early in the morning. When I came into "the knowledge of self" and the history of my people, everything shifted. Because of the impact to my spiritual nature, this historical and theological awakening came to me in college, although I was recruited to be a Commissioned Officer in The Army. I slammed on the breaks of proceeding to give my life to the Army, like the old ladies down South do, when attempting to avoid the "bad luck" omen, of a black cat crossing the road. I was convicted with a deeper knowing that I couldn't proceed, as I no longer felt that the Military was my safe place. Yet, I was full steam ahead with studying more about this country and truth that was hidden to me. It felt right for me at that time. However, it was *not* approved of by my family, especially those who supported me to pass all of the aptitude tests to be awarded the scholarship. As if that wasn't enough, I changed my religion. Shortly after, giving up my scholarship, I became a Muslim in the Nation of Islam. I felt like I belonged to something. Mind you, I had come to believe that I was already "the black sheep" in my family. I had located the source of the unworthiness script, which was fed by my young adult choices. This is key to connecting the dots of how unanswered childhood questions get filled in by many young adult choices, unconsciously. This was one of them, although I've always had a love affair with the Divine since very early in my childhood.

In my dedication to the religion, I later chose marriage as a natural next step, even before graduating college. Here again, was another young decision, disapproved of by my family. Yet, my unconscious determination to fill those gaps was set in motion. The challenges of being a young wife were many. The marriage lasted longer than most that start, while still young. I knew nothing about being a wife because I had no idea who I was as a woman, yet. After all, I was 19-years-old, growing up and growing into myself through religion. I can lovingly say that I was so naïve. I loved God. I dedicated myself to live a Godly life, in diet, dress, and decisions that aligned with that religion. Once again, those unanswered childhood questions resurfaced with every marital breakdown, personal struggle, and journal entry processing myself and my emotions. I was also young in leadership, in the Nation of Islam. That brought another level of resistance from women older than me, who I was given authority to directly oversee, if you will. So, when questions of my own womanhood and wifehood arose, I felt as if I had nowhere to go for advice. Here again, like the Christian women reluctant to come to my Pleasure Unplugged session, although they wanted to be supported, I was careful about who I opened up to.

Later, there were Elders and other friends in leadership that I peeled layers of learning beyond how to cook, how to clean, and how to act at home and abroad, as we were taught. There was more to being a woman and I was starting to feel it deep inside of me, with each life experience, including dreams deferred. While my ex-husband encouraged my development in any desire, I took on an identity that no longer aligned with the little girl looking for Daddy's love, unconsciously. It seemed more honorable to honor myself and my respect for him to release the marriage and answer another call. I was already growing weary of the religion and its translation of how my relationship with God should look.

Living in my truth was calling me with the stroke of my pen in my journal daily. Each truth that I told myself, explained the profuse fighting and my fatigue with feeling like something was wrong with me. We had grown apart. In fact, when we considered trying to conceive again, there was another voice screaming on the inside cautioning me. I'd gone to all of the appointments alone, even though it had been determined from the results with previous specialists that my fertility was NOT the issue. I was still taking it on, as if it was. I listened to that voice. I stopped my pursuit of conception. At that time, I didn't know that my womb was speaking, even then. Our womb speaks to us and we call it "something told me" or "intuition." This is the Power of Womb conversations, when we yield to it. Rather than focus on the marriage, I sought validation through my service in the mosque. He had his thing and I had mine and we both were good at it. Yet, the more personal development processes I engaged, after pain and disappointment inside those religious walls, I saw how much more I needed to do and I did exactly that. This was my first, SELAH Moment (a divine pause) of the future I had planned. It was a difficult end to the "good girl" and "good guy" love story. Yet, it was a new beginning of redefining what being a "good girl" meant for me, as a grown woman, not a little girl with a "Daddy's Girl" broken heart. Knowing what I know now, I see how it was possible to stay married and redefine, rebirth, and reinvent myself but I didn't have the skills to do so at the time.

I answered the call to transform my life, as I had known it. My rebirth began with answering the call of my womb for what I thought was conception when attending my very first Wonder Woman Workshop with Iyanla Vanzant, now known by the world for *Fix My Life*. I was 28-years-old when she asked me a question, that midwifed my process of rebirth long after I left her presence. In answering the question, "Can you be okay with yourself, if you never have a child?" broke me open. One answer revealed other answers that the young wife had never explored. It led me to the love I craved from my father and never being spoiled and cared for the way I experienced as a wife. I felt that had to give him something in return for all he was giving me, materially. I had become a kept woman, secured by a husband but never really felt secure as a little girl. This was the beginning of me developing those skills that allowed me to get honest about why I was married in the first place, the religion I chose, and all that I no longer aligned with me, as I matured and thought of myself in relation to my desires and dreams, prior to religious obedience. After all, I was in college and charting my own path, when I took literal the forecasts of doom and gloom. I began to ask myself, other questions about my choices to marry, when I remembered simple things like being invited to a rush for a sorority the weekend I got married. While I chose a good man as such a young girl, I must not have believed I alone was enough. This was the beginning of self-inquiry. The woman and the little girl began to have a relationship.

Fast forward, I moved in and out of self-discovery through relocation, religious resets, unsheltered from the world of dating and relationship. Almost, 10 years later my womb spoke again. Now, I'd become an Ordained Minister, Coach and Leader yet the residue of the "good girl" still had me making adult choices, unconsciously. This time a series of choices triggered by the death of my father, led me to seek and find the security of another man I thought was a "safe choice." Dating had not been kind to my heart. Mind you, I have had some time outside of religious restriction to discover more about myself and life. However, I should tell you what my turning point was. Like most matters in my life, it was a deep spiritual communication that was facilitated by my own womb. I was an Oracle to myself, before I stepped full into being that for others.

In 2005 my father died suddenly. I have written about impact of this death in a published compilation of stories, called "Still, Daddy's Girl." My Daddy's girl story had a happy ending, despite his sudden transition. We healed our relationship before he died. My work began to attract other "Daddy's Girls" who are healing through the deep trauma of a father's absence and their relationship with men. All of that spiritual work that I mentioned earlier was motivated by healing the beliefs, choices, and internal breakdowns as a result of unprocessed anger, fears of rejection and abandonment, and replacement of parental emotional availability with religion. Ah yes, I did my work in order to prepare to offer it to others. Iyanla and her team of wise women became Spiritual Mothers and wouldn't have it any other way. Mastery was required for the Inaugural Class of Inner Visions Institute and a demonstration of the ability to master aspects of your life and relationships.

Even though my relationship with my father was healed, my heart was broken again that he left so soon and I felt cheated. I was on a path that I was finally feeling confident about. He and I had developed an open communication and mutual respect. Yet, I feared I'd lose that respect had I told him, that the real reason I got robbed that night in Washington, DC was because I had collected all of my things from my boyfriend's and left in a fit of rage late that night. My sense of awareness was way off that night and at different points with this man. Unfortunately, that night didn't wake me up fully either. I eventually gather the scattered pieces of myself and my being enough. After exiting this toxic and occasionally abusive relationship, I purchased and moved into my own condo in under two months of my decision to exit that relationship (my dad or no one else knew, except for a few friends). It was a big deal to me and all of my friends who did know what I had concealed and toiled with for three years prior. I had stopped my life and refused invitations to Coach and Teach with a prestigious team who had mentored me for at least seven years. The day I moved the last of my things into the condo, I got the phone call: "La Tonia, your Daddy died." I do not even remember who was on the phone. I checked out from that day on October 2, 2005 for almost three years, until my womb spoke to tell me that was what happened.

With my things still in boxes, I had to depart to attend to my father's business. It was difficult for many reasons, that unfortunately too many families experience, when there is a death. I was disappointed with my father's siblings and I felt betrayed. I returned to very few local friends to support me, after months of supporting a leadership project with them. I learned lessons about people's ability to see the "strong one" breakdown. I share this, because it's relevant to all the choices I made while moving through a *"dark night of the soul."* It was necessary for me to grieve all of the years of other things I had never slowed down to grieve. Yet, I became involved in my life again with an appetite to "accomplish" things at a faster rate.

Submitting that piece about my father healed my heart. My capacity to love my father, beyond his limits taught me to trust the spiritual tools that I had been taught. It opened me to interact with my sacred circles again. I'd felt abandoned by my Dad, even in death and my circles while I grieved. It forced me to have deeper conversations with the same little girl, who wanted the validation and love of the masculine, I first knew, my Daddy. The death of a loved one can be an excruciating lonely place that I had not known prior to my Dad's departure. I wasn't juicy. So, I practiced a diet of forgiveness. Forgiveness restores your juices to flow, consciously. After all, my friends were no more insensitive than I had been prior to living this pain. It seemed natural to become *more* active in the pulpit. Yet, I see how I used religion as an escape, even then. Many of you know about this too. I needed grief therapy.

Instead, I started dating! The juicy option is conscious dating. I was not conscious, though. Sigh… In my mind, I was ready. The emphasis was on having and creating a family. There were good candidates from online dating and a couple of old flames who transitioned into friends with benefits. I never had an inner conversation of lack about my ability to attract a man. This was a gift from my mom and counsel of women who raised me. However, I had never allowed myself to be an investigator or connoisseur of men. At 19-years-old,

I was married. I had to learn how to date at 28-years-old after being married for 9 years to a wonderful man. I almost married and became a First Lady to a dear heart from my home state shortly after my relocation to DC. The distance wore us thin. Then, I continued to date, but not with intention and the mind of a JUICY woman. I had *Southern Girl values* and a *Modest Woman's Timelines* about anyone I saw as a potential husband. I was a serial monogamous and *that's* how I ended up in the relationship I had ended prior to my Dad's death. My mother will tell you that I wasn't always this way, because in my younger days I'd cut a man off in a heartbeat if he fucked up one time. I was OUT! Flight or fight was my self-protection mechanism, so liars were rather foreign to me, starting at a very young age. My first marriage didn't end with drama, lack of provision or because of cheating. That exit baffled folks because I was a kept woman, sheltered by the religious community. At least, it seemed so. Still I hated a lying ass man and made that clear in my choice to give myself "the gift of goodbye." That said, I still ended up with one (a lying ass man). Almost every woman will in this new world of dating. The only reason I stayed too long, hid the fights that turned physical, and ended my check and balance of snooping was because I told myself that I needed to apply The Universal Laws, Reality Creation Tools and exceptional understanding of The Law of Attraction to heal the reason I had attracted this relationship. I over-corrected. This can happen to those of us who have been conditioned by religion to take things literally. It is fed by the belief that, "If I do this, then I'll get _____." There is some truth to this; however there was more truth to know.

There was more to learn about myself, as a result of losing a parent. I was just beginning to feel strong enough to write my book, travel the word teaching and healing, and prosper in business. I had wanted both of my parents to "see me" accomplish certain goals. Now, I had one parent to hear me preach, see my name in lights, hold my first child, and just be proud of me. So, when my next candidate for a husband came around, I didn't see that my inner program and timeline was speaking louder than good sense. Sometimes, we make permanent decisions for temporary situations. I kicked into high gear after being courted and was convinced that this was a good thing. You see, my first voice, told me, "This country boy is not for you," but he was nice. I even believed that he was *safe*, and I was fatigued from all of the disappointment from previous misfires. However, I was not conscious of this. Despite my better judgment, I proceeded, anyway. Unfortunately, it was three years, more lies, several break-ups, the selling of my condo, and many SELF-betrayals later, that I was in deep, so I told my ego. I knew better than to proceed, because I saw and experienced moment after moment of lies and distrust to KNOW for certain.

"When you seek permission for pleasure, then you know you have been programmed for pain! Operating system upgrade required!" —**Taylor Made Inspirations**

Self-betrayal starts with small acts, outside of your own self honor. The moment I found his ex's phone number and confirmation that he was indeed at her house, was the first one. The moment of hanging out with the phone ringing off the hook, people knocking on the window and being called a bitch, while being thrown across the bed when I tried to answer, would be enough. Or maybe, after attending the funeral of his father only to see the woman behind the phone calls, walk in with the family, while I sat on the side. I thought that I was taking a high road to be there for him. Remember, I had been conditioned to have a very literal approach to my application of spiritual truth. So, when he returned after the funeral, begged to be restored to my good graces and explained why I was handled with such disrespect, I forgave him. I mean, wasn't that what I had been taught to do? Forgive others. I told myself that I'd monitor myself closely, while being there for a friend who had just lost his father a couple of weeks before the anniversary of my own father's death. I mean, I couldn't leave him, the way I felt others had left me. So, I allowed him in my space only to lie about too many things to write. There were many justifiable moments to leave and never look back, from hiding an entire shared cell phone account, large gifts purchased by this woman, to her driving to his house from another State to reclaim the key to her house and one after the other. Each one of these occurrences were met with justifications and explanations, no woman of my spiritual gifts and understanding should have tolerated past the first occurrence. But I did. I married it. Perhaps, I thought it was some form or atonement and restitution, because he was a gentle soul who allowed himself to be bullied by The Ex-Wife,

The Baby's Mother and The Old Injured friend. It was a trilogy of toxic relating that affected his child support and I told myself to love like a true Christian. This is also the version I heard. My journey to become JUICY opened me and removed layers, I didn't know existed.

The Spiritual Life Coach in me had been trained by Masters. The woman with so much love to give was ready to have what she wanted (a family) and had the tools to manifest it. The *Southern Good Girl* wanted upward mobility. I had activated it already in my own life. That condo I worked so hard to acquire was intended to be a rental property. I attended to debt and paid them off. My coaching business and ministry engagements were thriving. I loved myself and felt really good about my life, despite still grieving. I believed that my love could heal and compensate for the trespasses against me. So, I proceeded and accepted the "good behavior" that my future husband offered for an extended period of time to demonstrate his good intention. I derailed my plans to purchase a beautiful home in Upper Marlboro, Maryland, that I was pre-approved to purchase and even moved my furniture into storage awaiting the loan to clear from the family selling. He convinced me that we could have more, bigger, and better together. I accepted the offer in good faith and purchased a dream home an hour away in *"The Ranch Club,"* a Maryland suburb with Country Club like amenities. Next, I planned a small wedding that I thought would make my mother happy, since I didn't have one with my first marriage. After all, I had one parent now, so I held internal pressure to get certain things done so she could "see" me have all of the things that she often said she wanted for her girls. I wanted my mother to have this moment for herself, so I walked down the aisle knowing that I was in *waaay* too deep. Now, I had skills to manifest my vision that I didn't have earlier as a wife, searching for herself.

"There are three kinds of healing methods. One Involves suffering, and another involves pain, and the last involves pleasure. The first is exemplified by chemotherapy; the second, by surgery; and the third, by sexual healing positions."—The Alchemy of Horus and the Sex Magic of Isis

My journey to become JUICY continued to whisper to me. Little did I know I had found myself and then lost her again. A part of the whisper to press forward despite my knowing was the desire to have children. Quite naturally, I resumed my investigation of why I hadn't begun the next phase of becoming pregnant. You'd think with an active sex life, I would have had some accidents along the way. Nope. I've never seen an abortion clinic and only have miscarried once that I know of in my first marriage. So, I needed to know why my womb had betrayed me too. After each doctor's appointment alone, I returned to my car full of emotion, and alone. Each time the doctor stirred around in my womb, it released a floodgate of either emotions or deeper conversations about myself. I started to call my sister, after each appointment, and she comforted me or asked me more questions, which caused me to go deeper into emotions and conversations about myself. Some of the procedures were painful to bear. I should not have been alone, yet like in most things, I didn't know how to ask for support. My female fertility specialist was matter of fact, with little compassion. I sat in waiting rooms reading the numerous brochures of coaches and support groups who specialized in offering support to women and spouses. Mine was at work and rather oblivious that something was stirring in me until the last appointment. The last appointment is when *my womb spoke* to me. The Surgeon confirmed that there were eight tiny fibroids that he would not normally bother. Most of them were embedded in my wall of my uterus and wouldn't stop conception. However, there was one that sat right inside the uterus that was blocking conception and causing me excruciating ovulation pain. The Surgery would remove this one, the others, and reposition my left ovary. I felt ready and resolved to "just do it." In hindsight, I wish that I had accessed other resources because I definitely had plenty of resources, given the company I kept knowledgeable with every healing modality you could imagine. Plus, fertility was not a new quest for me. I wanted children with my first husband, went to a specialist, a Traditional Asian Naturopath and studied every book written on womb health and herbs. I conceived and miscarried in the first trimester. The little old man practicing this ancient healing modality taught me, after I returned the connection between the womb and the energy of a woman. I had gotten upset and he was able to sense that in my post care. This is what led me to become Certified in Iridology (study of the eyes for imbalances in the body), Nutritional Health, Reiki, and just good ole' mama earth practices. Here again, I knew better than to accept Allopathic (Modern Western Medicine) trained "practice" of medicine.

However, all of this other knowledge was also my way of taking shortcuts and neglecting myself. These weeks in and out of doctor's offices had really made me face these truths. On this final verdict, I drove down the Baltimore-Washington Parkway hearing the confirmation that something was off. The gift of empathic knowing was active again. It is JUICY to trust your inner voice concerning your health and desires. Often times, the voice of other authorities are louder and more weighed than our own. We've been taught to go to the doctor rather than nature, ours and The Earth's. Mind you, I had been telling my OB GYN this for years but she'd dismiss me and tell me, "Oh you're fine," with no further investigation. My good girl, former Muslim and reformed Christian had chosen a good girl, Christian doctor who didn't believe I should be having sex, much less having a baby anyway. So, I didn't push. Nor did I press on to a second opinion. I remained a loyal patient with her year after year, and year after year, I hear the Voice get louder. It said, *"This is what you do, La Tonia. You are loyal to everybody, except yourself."* I almost veered off of the road, except the collision with myself was happening inside instead of in my lovely luxury vehicle on the way to my luxurious home. I'm sure you can relate to having things appear so nice on the outside, yet on the inside something else is happening. Instead of pulling over, I drove and cried. I wept for not listening to myself. I cried as I took inventory of organizations, concepts, and years of dedication to causes that I had been loyal too. Then, the husband called, and I told him the unedited truth about how I knew better to be with him. He dismissed it as me just "bitching." Self-betrayal is the real bitch. Having my sexuality and womanhood connected exclusively to a man was the real bitch. The unconscious realization that I'd done this again shook me to my core. Here I was clearing the way for pregnancy, so I thought only to open the way for me and my womanly truth.

That was another, SELAH moment!

I needed support. You'd think I would call the obvious core circle of phenomenal women around me. My mind went blank. Certain ones that I would call would require too much of the back story to understand the weight of what I was carrying, like a secret pregnancy. By this time, I already had the wedding, the house warming, and everyone thought I was living inside of my dream. I'd only confessed my truth to my best friend in Chicago and my cousin. My best friend and I had done significant self-development work together and Goddess study, so she knew how to hold space, as a Goddess. We studied and practiced these Goddess Arts together and exchanged resources. She was the one who counseled me just before my class reunion trip, when I knew I'd see my childhood sweetheart with whom I had unfinished emotional business or fantasy of "unfinished" emotional business. My cousin picked up where Charise left off because we always held each other's truth in confidence, and she was my road dog at the reunion. This was a truth unleashed from my womb, which would require more work from me now. On this long ride home from the doctor's office, I reached out to a Coach that my Reverend Sister had done great work with and I had started earlier. She said to me rather direct and without much compassion, "*This truth that you are now aware of, demands your action. You had better decide for yourself that you will address it or next time something may grow inside of you that they won't be able to cut out."* Sometimes that's how a dark energy rides in us, blinds us, and plugs our ears so that we cannot see. JUST. LIKE. THAT. I wailed for the unconscious coma I had been in that got me here after I hung up the phone.

A deeper work began from that day! My womb continued to reveal to me my relationship with the feminine I spoke to it as well. I asked questions about what the fibroids represented, what dreams had been unborn and what old hurts had lodged themselves there. I studied more and hired a therapist. I knew the marriage was over before it started. I had buyer's remorse for both the husband and the house. So much was on the line. I had become the liar that I hated. So, my first order of business was to tell the truth. I outed myself. I told the truth to my sister, my prayer partners, my sister-friends, my Pastor (also my dear friend) and finally my mother. I was scared of her judgment and more poor advice to just stay, because he is a "good man, who goes to work every day." I told my sister how I had taken advice from my mother regarding this entire marriage, in the first place. She was shocked because we knew that some of our mom's views about men and marriage weren't a match for our own. Yet, my sister and every woman I outed myself to held a space of love and non-judgment. The *outing* process was necessary. My prayers reached deep into communion with my womb and my foremothers. My prayer tongue was no longer edited because I *outed* myself in my prayers about my relationship and messages about "all things mother" and could now reach into a trance-like surrender. Here is where the magic of being a woman happens. It's not sexual, yet very connected to a woman's sexuality. My prayers became specific and deeper. The God of my understanding, the mother in me. God, my relationship with my mother ordered my steps. My womb prayers would guide me to each practitioner I needed pre- and post-surgery. As a metaphysical minister, I knew of the mind and body connection. Therefore, I prepared myself to release the belief, patterns, and self-denial that created these fibroids. I went into surgery clearer than the three years prior where I told myself one thing and did another.

When your Master Teachers hold you accountable the way mine did, I was clear that I was in an accountability season and if I didn't get these lessons for my womanhood, I would repeat them. In other words, it would be a different pair of pants offering the same Special Ed curriculum. I was alone but I didn't have to be. I was blind and now was finally awake. So, after weeks of bed rest and restoration, I returned to therapy, reflexology, nature, coaching, and energy work, transparent conversations with my circle and to The Goddess. I faced my Mother Wound, also. For so long, it had been about my father. A desire for an orgasmic and healed womb led me from one resource to another, where no declarations were made except to get to the bottom of "how I got here." Mind you, that "I" in how I got here was loaded on the weight of being a Coach, Minister and Healer. How did "I" get here? Well, one of my Reverend Sisters said, "The answer lives in the same room as the question." Partnership with my womb and heart healing held answers for me, and one day in a therapy session, my counselor asked me one question about my father and the timing of his death.

It opened me, like Iyanla's question did years prior, except it didn't take as long to get to the answer. That 'Aha!' moment moved mountains from my sight and bricks from my Astral body. I saw the connection to my choices. My reaction: It's that childhood shit again?

While I was relieved on one hand to finally know, the coach in me understood that with knowledge comes responsibility. I (my subconscious mind) created and attracted this opportunity for healing! Unconsciously, I had conjured exactly what I wanted and masterminded with myself to have one spiritual bypass after another in order to have my "good girl" vision turn-out. Was this courage or cowardice? I think it was a mixture of both. After all, I told myself that my small family flew into town for this wedding, we had a mortgage now, my niece was in college nearby and the financial impact would impact her comfort. She was in my care and deserved to be comfortable. I couldn't make a sudden move, so I didn't. I stayed in therapy, prayed, and listened for the release. I knew that I would *just know* when the release happened. The study of pleasure amplified my restoration and courage to conjure my return to a "presence" not too far in the future or getting stuck in the past. My husband and I were not sleeping in the same bed, but I wasn't the least bit upset about it. Ending the obligation to be sexual outside of my desire was the beginning of my womanly recovery and my yoni falling in love with me again.

Dedication was now to my mental health, physical restoration and joy, and pleasure healed me drop by drop in a six-month program that began four-months prior at a women's conference in Miami. I made the largest investment in myself that I'd ever made, outside of purchases of a house and car with no money and no job. My temporary disability was running out shortly, but honey chile, don't you know… everything flowed when my juices streamed inside of me, where I felt like the blood in my veins were running at a rapid speed upward throughout my body to the top of my head. I literally felt dizzy, yet transcendent. I'll never forget writing the check at the end of that Miami weekend, trembling yet trusting the Universe to supply my needs and my desire.

Now being fully present with myself in a new way, I started to feel excited about my next steps and I moved toward them with confident expectation of special delivery. I returned to work in a position that seemed to be prepared just for me. I resumed coaching with a new understanding of the power of this sacred portal, called *"pussy,"* after this experience. It was a word that I was no longer ashamed to use in reference to my spirituality. Saying the "P" word had been inappropriate to use, except with my girlfriends talking about adult things. The words used to describe womanhood by men have profane meanings, now had been clarified to mean something altogether different. My juices flowed and my power of the *pussy* was so far beyond "service" to everyone else. In other words, it was not just a word I used to be naughty with men or speak naughty with my girls. No more. I opened to the power of my yoni as Divinity. Yoni is another Sanskrit word meaning sacred flower that I use to elevate my reference to this seat of power; I was gifted. My juice was in service to myself. Being in a relationship with my Yoni meant having ownership of myself in a deeper way, something I had only read about in previous years. Whether one calls it Womb, Yoni or Pussy Power, it became a Divine Counsel that ordered every step I would take on her behalf. I listened deeper to myself and honored myself by being in the company of other turned-on women, who were tapped into this specialized knowing, often called Goddess. I re-engaged aspects of my life that I had not given myself the space and time to enjoy, such as trips with my sisters, football with friends and quality "girl" time. You know how we tend to stop our lives when we get in a relationship? Yeah. I wasn't doing that anymore, nor was I coaxing him to attend my speaking engagements or travel any longer. I became enough for me to live in my overflow from things that brought me joy, made me laugh and inspired me to dance. There was a turning point for me, while in New Orleans, a city I consider my heart-town. It was on the Dowman Bridge in New Orleans for the Super Bowl, that I heard, "You are released. You can leave now. You are clear." It came from deep within. It was juicy, in a powerful way. I trusted the juicy in my power without question. I wasn't angry with him and I confess it took me a very long time, even after I left, to not be angry at myself. Whew!

In fact, it took another turn. I could feel myself, again. Those sacrifices that I became aware of during my post-surgery recovery inspired me to pay attention to my desires and cravings that I'd never explored. I started to audit my wardrobe by enjoying things I'd never done, taking trips to indulge my pleasure to tantalize my senses. My pleasure became my center references to move the pain. I started to LIVE and have fun with me and my sensuality. Therefore, I did not stay in the anger with myself for sustained periods of time. Pleasure in spirit, pleasure in my work, pleasure in my love, and pleasure in my money, would drive me closer to what I believed about pain, struggle or deprivation. Prior to exploring my wholeness through pleasure, I had known value through achievement and "going hard" for the thing I wanted to achieve. Achievement taught me early on how to perform well and work hard. I called it discipline. Being disciplined kept me from being disciplined by others, so I learned how to secure myself through serious focus in almost all aspects of my life. Choosing pleasure required another kind of discipline incentivized by following my bliss. That required me to pay closer attention to relaxing and giving myself permission to define that moment by moment, day by day and new experience. I loved myself enough to face my starved, cravings in love, sex and money. What did I really desire became a check-in point versus what seemed practical and logical? I was outside of my comfort zone, which was unconsciously a very masculine way of being in the world. It can open any woman to test her limits, only to find more of God there, in the feminine, not less. It stretched the mind to choose this level of feminine integration. Why? Because being a woman has been so defined by other people or institutions. Being a turned on and juicy black woman who trusted the softer edges of my feminine as a source of power offered another type of knowing. Being Juicy, does not exempt us from experiencing pain, while filling our container of self-care, desire, and joyful self-discovery with pleasure that co-exists with the spiritual, sexual, and fulfillment. I loved me enough to stay in the motion of authenticity and stewardship, despite finding places where I needed to forgive myself from former self-betrayal. The moment I communicated truthfully and in depth to my soon to be ex-husband at the time, I rebirthed another level of spiritual integrity. I put my "big girl" panties on, taking responsibility for my life, beyond a victim, owning my participation, even at the subconscious level. Even though, ownership and responsibility were not new concepts to me from the leadership perspective, Spiritual Responsibility as a tool for transformation offered a different access point to understand laws that govern The Universe. I create my reality had new meaning, even though I read it and passed the exams that tested my coaching knowledge. It was intellectual. There were unconscious core beliefs that made me default to making sure that I didn't get in trouble. Pleasing an "external" God, made it easy to focus on external authority in several aspects of my relationships and ways of relating to the world. Perhaps, the shift from being a "good girl" who worries about pleasing others, even a God "out there" verses honoring the God within, and into the big girl panties that doesn't allow blame, shame or guilt to claim her power. The good girl had become masterful at making choices rooted in what I wanted to avoid or not experience, like addiction and drugs, abortion and pregnancy or a bad reputation. As outspoken and passionate as I was, the little girl relationship that I had with myself needed to facilitate my own inner authority. Some call this being unapologetic for who you are. I felt it deeper. To be unapologetic can have an undertone grounded in the Ego by spiritual definitions. In this Goddess movement, I hear the term unapologetic often. That's not what my feminine curriculum assigned it. I call it *"feminine atonement,"* when a woman doesn't need Ego because she is enough without a facade of strength or freedom, for that matter. In the atoned place, a woman has nothing to prove, not even to God. Pleasure opened me to know more of God's love in, around and through me. Sensuality is a gateway to open the senses. I walked through every one only to find new invitations to myself and self-mastery. This is the power of pleasure that I know through the breakthrough and divine set-ups that followed to confirm my decision and resolve. Just in case I should have any doubt in myself, this new way of being attuned from my core not anyone else's. The benefits of my juicy activation far outweighed the restraints defined by other people, including those who had interpreted what "being good" meant for being a "good woman" for someone else.

My Lesson:

The power of our womb is often limited to child-bearing, pleasing a partner, and a menstrual cycle by the culture conditioning and layers of our inherited beliefs along each woman's journey. But, it is more. The womb speaks to every woman. We have not been taught to pay attention unless we are in physical pain or ridiculous surface-level pleasure. At this time, prior to my surgery, my Tantra studies taught me the power of our womb beyond an orgasm. Tantra in Western culture is often watered-down and commercialized to simply be about sexual positions and chasing an orgasm. I'm grateful that Tantra practices ushered into a deeper communication with the Divine for me. Healing is required to make room for physical orgasm, as well as the mental, emotional, and spiritual orgasms.

Naturally, my life became more and more orgasmic, even while I continued to recover from the blows of self-betrayal that my ego had covered. Responsibility at this level is not intended to be a burden carried as a point of reference for guilt and shame. Responsibility at this level is having a commitment to healing that becomes a launching pad for the emancipation of your womanhood. The definition of pleasure expanded as my feminine responsibility matured and I trusted the collection of deposits to live a vision that a Living Goddess deserves.

Juicy Journal Exercise:

What parts of my journey can you see in your own?

Where have you ignored your own inner guidance system and proceeded anyway?

What decisions did you make about your life, once you realized it - if you did?

What have you done to begin to restore and/or rebirth your life?

Chapter 2 : Juicy Nudges

"The very thing that you think is WRONG with you is exactly what's RIGHT, UNIQUE, ASSIGNED "ONLY" to YOU! Start blessing what you've been cursing and make room for it to bless you."
—Taylor Made Inspirations

Now, let's fast forward to sharing my Juiciness with others. Remember, I had always been known, amongst close friends, for loving to talk sexual things. While talking to my friend Charise, about teaching on the spiritual aspects of pleasure, I declared, "I'm a Juicy Spirit!" The more I played with my own limits and push past them; I began to write what I was hearing directly from Spirit about the intersection of the Spiritual and Sexual, specifically for the feminine soul. While it felt new, it wasn't. I had forgotten, much like my sister circle, that this was not new for me. I had a library of spiritual resources inside of me from my previous spiritual references, including orgasm. I had bedside books that I'd selected to support me in being a "good wife" who satisfied my husband because I knew very little about satisfying myself as a 19-year-old wife, even though I enjoyed sex. I had already been collecting pieces of this puzzle long before I knew that this was "a thing," a real thing in the world of Spirituality. In one of my personal study halls, I returned to my writing. Then, I found this piece I had written for my sister circle stored in my electronic files:

THE MESSAGE OF THE WISHBONE

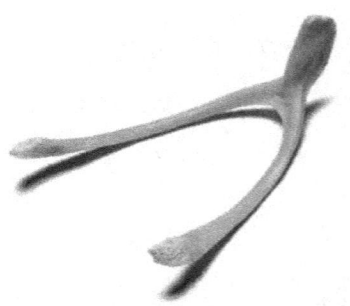

[wishes granted]

When I wrote this in October 2007, I shared it with a small circle of friends I believed wouldn't judge me. I couldn't reconcile this ministry of pleasure, bliss, and sensuality as being "acceptable" by the mainstream. In truth, I was still conforming and containing my own pleasure. This post is an activation of my creativity, abundance, and passion in trusting the Universe to make room for my gifts—gifts that I literally had been sitting on. Today on January 1, 2011, I share my first blog post, affirming that *"I am safe to be and express a pleasure-filled blueprint as a healer, student, and teacher."* **Are you sitting on your gifts?** If you are a woman, I submit an EMPHATIC, "YES!" You are sitting on your gifts and it is a part of both your physical and spiritual anatomy.

A couple of nights ago, I was watching a program called The Anatomy of Sex. I believe it was on Discovery Health. I learned something new and very useful. In fact, I learned something very spiritual. The clitoris is shaped like a WISHBONE. Many of us have been taught to think of "only" the small pearl shaped organ, covered by the hood. Nope, the nerve endings create the shape of a wishbone that creates angelic waves of orgasmic pleasure beyond our vulvas! Think about that! Therefore, this organ is designed for pleasure at various points in the body. What "they" explained on this documentary is that vaginal orgasms are a myth. It's really the clitoris being stimulated or rubbed at certain spots during intercourse that create various levels of orgasmic energy. However, I know and other experts will tell you, that vaginal orgasms are NOT a myth at all. There are several areas of orgasmic release in the womb temple. We could really "go there" on those deeply, pleasurable, juicy releases and their messages but that not my point though!

Back to the wishbone! I was thinking about us as women and what we've been taught to believe or disbelieve about pleasure, being pleasing and/or the mask of pleasantries. While digesting the science of pleasure, it becomes evident how dogma has conditioned many through religion to be removed from the full embrace of our sexuality and pleasure. When we study the history of cultures prior to Constantine, many communities were sexually free. To experience the Kundalini energy was a high spiritual experience. Today, it still is. Don't you know oh so well that when we are in the throes of pleasure, we say, "Oh God!" or we simply breathe deeply? It's called the HA breath. The HA or Ah is the translation for the names of God. Even when in the worship experience, Hallelujah is the highest praise. This sound can be found no matter the name we call God, Goddess, or all that is. My point is that this indeed is that sexual/sensual pleasure, a high spiritual experience, when held in higher esteem coupled with deliberate surrender.

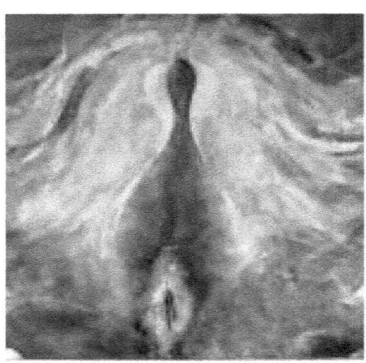

Your body holds many more roadmaps than this.

Back to the wishbone! Pleasure for a woman is her seat of power. It is her creative power. When we study the Law of Creation, appropriately named, there are some signals to our spiritual power. The Law of Creation is also known as the Law of Attraction, recently made famous by the movie *The Secret*. The Law of Creation (a/k/a attraction) simply says, "Whatever you put your attention on expands." Yes, EXPANDS! **What wishes would you like to expand?** This one law became popular, although there are several (7-9) core Universal Laws that all work together and can be found in the Esoteric teaching of Jesus. In other words, it's supported by scripture, therefore, those that "need" it now have permission to make room for pleasure. As a metaphysician, I always love *going into the deeper meaning*, no pun intended here. Metaphysics is the term used to study that which is beyond the physical, beyond what we can touch, see, taste, and feel.

The Universal Laws are the non-physical principles that govern our Universe in an unfailing, impartial, consistent, and dependable fashion. I'll have to get back to this, if you need me to.

Back to the wishbone! So, as we focus on our *pleasure*, allowing *pleasure* and embracing *pleasure* in our lives, we become more powerful to attract a/k/a create the lives we want. We become magnets for our manifestation. *What if* we taught women to be selective or celibate because of "this" truth and power rather than punishment, guilt, and shame? *What if* we knew this was a seat of power and when we auction it off mindlessly, it depletes our ability to be attractive to the very desires we have. *What if,* we were taught to use our sexual pleasure to manifest and worship the Divinity within? *What if,* we took our wishbone out of the mental and emotional prisons our core beliefs have created? Whether single or married… *What if,* we knew that our pleasure is a secret accelerator or a tool to open the gates to usher us into manifesting our vision?

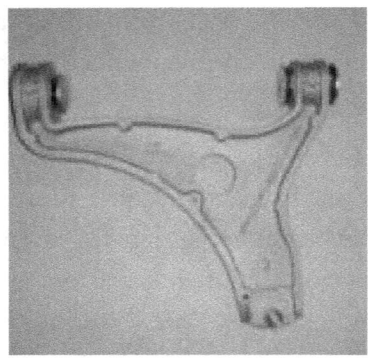

This is the power of The Goddess (God Is). This gift is a gateway. It is our portal to open the way to our desires, which takes me back to the Law of Attraction:

Inspirational speaker, Esther Hicks reminds us in her work to…

1) **Ask** – This is a feminine demonstration of receptivity. So many of us have forgotten or never used the muscle of "asking" for anything. We are asking consciously or unconsciously all the time, anyway. In Matthew 7:7, "Ask and it will be given to you; seek and you will find; knock and the door will be opened to you."

2) **The Universe Answers** – This part is not our job. This is where it may look like we need to "do" something. Control freaks may have to find a new fetish. In other words, this is where we must surrender and practice detachment

from the outcome, while raising our expectation. We always get what we've asked for – conscious or unconscious also! In Matthew 11:24, "Therefore I tell you, whatever you ask for in prayer, believe that you have received it, and it will be yours."

3.) **Allow** – This is our work to align with what we've asked for and our internal G.P.S. has answered. So, by the time it manifests, it's only evidence of our alignment. Did you get that? It is EVIDENCE of what is already ours. In Habakkuk 2:2-3, "Then the Lord answered me and said: Write the vision, and make it plain on tables, that he may run who reads it. For the vision is yet for an appointed time, but at the end it will speak, and it will not lie: though it tarries, wait for it; because it will surely come, it will not tarry."

This is the breakdown for many of us, well at least it was for me. **So, back to the wishbone!** Living an orgasmic life and embracing our desires via pleasure creates a cycle, a wave or vibration. The pleasure (fun, creativity, play, flirting, receiving compliments, orgasm, fulfillment of purpose) supports us in the 'allowing' process. This is where the connection lies to setting the other laws in motion.

- The Law of Detachment (aka the Law of Allowing) says that in order to intentionally attract something, we must relinquish our attachment to it. This is the surrender! The trust! During the orgasm process there is detachment from reality as endorphins are released for our good.

- The Law of Unlimited Potential (aka the Law of Pure Potentiality) says that we are unlimited children of a very prosperous, powerful, omnipotent, impartial, all-providing, all-sufficient, all-loving Father/Mother/God. This is using our imagination (vision/meditation), especially in sex. We can have it before we have it.

- The Law of Reciprocity (aka the Law of Giving) says that as you give you shall receive. Give and forgive. Intimacy requires engagement of all parties, in an out of the sexual experience.

- The Law of Cause and Effect says for every action, there is an equal and opposite reaction. Reaping and sowing in your own life. The effects of becoming cause of your own orgasm are juicier, than focusing on someone else being the cause of your orgasm.

So, Ladies… remember your wishbone is MUCH MORE than just anatomy. Your anatomy represents access points of pleasure, purpose and passion, mind, body and spirit. Our anatomy is perfectly designed like a multilayered wishbone. This message that I held all those years blessed me to open to my senses, my desires, and confirmed my own process of relaxing into the joy of being a woman and following my bliss.

Consider that as you read this book. Consider your own resistance. Girlhood feeds Womanhood and women choose to be a Goddess. I had chosen well, perhaps even in another lifetime. Now, when I sing the song "God Is," I hear a different reminder, which is "God is. Therefore, I am." Consider what you have been choosing as a result of your womanly relationship with life, intimacy, truth-telling and savoring all of the flavors of your life and yourself as a woman. Make a wish and use your anatomy to open the way.

Juicy Journal Truth:

What words have you used for your "lady parts"?

How have you defined pleasure?

When and where do you express your sensuality?

What would you do more of if you weren't worried about what others think of you?

Do you have a vision for sensuality? If so, how would you use it to create and connect other parts of your life that you may have compartmentalized?

Chapter 3: Why Juicy?

"Being in personal possession of yourself, your shadow and your light is to be AWAKENED, Turned-On and JUICY!" —**Taylor Made Inspirations**

The context of being JUICY conjures the experience of biting into a ripe piece of fruit and just as you bite into it, other juices and flavors are released, squirting its deliciousness inside and outside of your mouth. This fruit leaves your hands, mouth, and maybe your clothes with evidence of this explosion of nature's sappy, sweet essence all over the one who partakes. Juicy evokes a sense of gratitude for being the recipient of all who get the abundance contained behind this outer layer, not to mention how it energizes you. Juicy is an energy or a power, like getting juice when a car battery died or electric power lines that give us lights in our homes and offices. Pleasure has this type of power, of the fruit, the nutrients from the fruit and the energetic boost to generate or regenerate our cells. Sensuality is powerful in this way. We have been conditioned to respect it or fear it. Many western women have forgotten how to use this as a service to their spirit and their healing.

Two previous marriages, a familiar relationship with rejection, struggling with religiosity, and my own spirituality, I had denied my juiciness through my willful compliance. I had been conditioned to be a "Good Girl," a black "Southern Bell," a "Virtuous Woman" and/or any other rule abiding woman. I was pregnant with freedom and a ministry of liberation that had revealed itself to me in my own process of cocooning then breaking free, level by level of new understanding. After all I studied, I was teachable and coachable at every level, until I reached the feminine activation of my own DNA guiding me through my womanhood demand *to know*. I discovered in my answering a soul call for freedom, that for quite some time I was trapped in a cocoon, wanting to break free and take flight as the beautifully liberated butterfly that I am. There was defining moment in my womanhood, that I attribute to the fierce leadership of an older woman, named Rita, sent into my life to help me to see how I was still cocooning. This woman later became a Godmother, on my personal board of trustees. She and I were hanging out and she was telling me about my body type. I may have said something like, "*I don't have no figure.*" And, she read me up one side and down the other. She said, "Come here." We went into her bedroom where she started pulling clothes out for me to try on. I think she asked me a question about sizes. I didn't really know but the size I gave to her was too big. She read me some more, with love but explanation about fitting clothes to my body and why. I did not know my own bra size. My clothes were still too big after years of being a Muslim woman who stylishly covered. This represented my hiding on so many levels, because I was a skinny stick in my school days and developed an insecurity with all the girls who had full bottoms that Southern men absolutely love. My self-esteem took the blow of comparing myself very early. So, it was easy to go into a religion and wear a lot of fabric. Unfortunately, years later when I was depressed and emotionally eating I gained weight as a result of this fabric and didn't realize how big I had gotten until the weight set in uncomfortably. So, all of my clothes post-divorce, relocation, and an exodus from the mosque later in DC were too big. Therefore, I had a left-over wardrobe that I didn't have a budget to change, nor the consciousness. This was not JUICY, y'all!

That day, Mama Rita mothered me where I didn't know I needed it. She affirmed my figure, my height, and demonstrated how I could style myself to compliment all of it. I did exactly that, layer by layer my wardrobe began to change. It felt good in the land of juicy self-discovery, after NOT knowing Juicy for so long. Getting to know my body, my proper bra size, and my taste was gradual. After adhering to codes of modesty, discovering just how juicy my body and Amazonian stature was took time. Even though I was updating the outside, it began within. Being a juicy woman begins with body positivity. Often the voices in our head do not match the true presentation of our beauty.

The journey to becoming JUICY has to begin somewhere. It was an unlearning process and a learning that expanded my preferences and expression. I recognize that not only do I have options, I have seasons. What I choose in one season was not to be confined. I can choose again. My wardrobe symbolized that. In one season, I moved from the signature religious attire that covered me, to business suits with more form fitting tops and lower neck-lines, to dresses for parties, to discover I had legs. I adored my long seductive legs, again with the help of a sister while preparing for pleasure-centered workshop/getaway. I still have that short pink swing dress today. That was a turning point for my JUICY. I had pushed through an outer skin and bit down into my own fruit to find a nectar inside me that I wanted more of.

After years of compliance to a religion and layers of other internalized messages about being a God-fearing woman, I no longer chose to live in a fear-based relationship with God. My ministerial preparation allowed me to study scriptures, research, and interpret so-called sacred text for myself first. I may have thought that I was doing it as a part of the curriculum. However, we all have a spiritual curriculum the moment we are birthed here on earth. We tend to default and drop out of the course of study, if we had custodians (parents) who did the same as a result of survival mode and inherited models for living. This doesn't reduce their doing the best they knew how, nor is it an indictment on our parents. It is a necessary observation of their limitations, so you can make new choices to transcend them. It all serves a high purpose in your life to be the change they prayed for or create a new way of being. In my seminary year, I had already chosen the butterfly, as the symbol for Rebirth International, my ministry and marketplace endeavors; I was in a process. I knew I was on a precipice of my spreading my own wings. Rebirth was certain to be an interruption, a bridge for me into me. It said that "intimacy" really means "into-me-I-see." Pleasure, seduction, and sensuality are often known for its use in intimacy with another living being. This intimacy was bursting me open to find deliciousness there. Because of this, I've been able to hold other women's hand at their crossroads of sensual self-discovery. For some women, if it's not your wardrobe, it could be another part of yourself that you're hiding, restricting or over-exposing, for that matter. Any extreme relationship with our senses, our succulence and/or our turn on can be reviewed. Women who are codependent on their exterior, image or body type can have the same breakthrough, in reverse. The point is to be willing to push through the limit or attachment.

We have to allow ourselves flexibility to change. This was my lesson and message from my own life to Rebirth and emerge transformed, by choice and deliberate action. As I fast forward into my juicy rebirth, I held an emerging vision and saw this for the program that would liberate other women who wanted to spread their butterfly wings around the world. There are plenty of options from teachers who offer the techniques of blow jobs, squirting orgasms, improved relationships from the yin muscle and radical relating, as the leader. I saw it different because it was different for me. I began chasing improved "orgasm" with the best of them and built my own repertoire of techniques. I never bore of technique talk, but the women who came to me wanted something deeper. Heck, some were more proficient at techniques than I, as former strippers and dancers to confirm that they too wanted more. Both wanted to heal the division that imprisoned a part of their healing. The sensual nectar of a woman heals and frees her to be medicine to her own feminine soul. Just like my wardrobe, my

Juicy Spirit evolved into a sensual transformative experience, as a bridge for the woman on either side of the extreme - Juicy and Spiritual or Juicy as Spiritual.

Why stay with JUICY, though? I could have called it anything safe, given the flip-side of the results I found from Pleasure Unplugged to a few rounds of Juicy Spirit, which was fear. I outright heard from the women who were so elated to have enrolled that they worried about what people would think enrolling in or inviting it to their platform. When I started, there may have been others but I didn't know many of them in my circles. I even had one sensual practitioner explain to me how many years it took for her to be taken seriously, as she specialized in educating women on their own anatomy and orgasm. When medical conferences started to invite her, she could then support herself by doing what she loved. I give thanks for the forerunners of sensual teachers. Unfortunately, not many of them look like me. Women who look like me need this the most due to the historical burden melaninated women have carried throughout the ages of women's history. Despite the fear, woman who had grown tired of playing it safe came to me. I found that the only risk they chose was the one they were taking on their authentic self. ***Juice is defined as a person's vitality or creative faculties and the informal definition says to "juice something up" is to enliven it or make it lively. The word "spirit" is a noun, verb, and an adjective. As a noun it is the vital principle in humans, animating the body or mediating between body and soul. Ironically, as a verb it means to encourage, stir up or action.***

While talking vitality, potency, and the power of JUICY began in a serious way for me. It was all fun using the tools taught in the Rites of Passage process, that balanced and lifted me and others to recognize themselves, as the woman worthy to witness her own sweetness. Learning to play, skip, hop, get naked, dance in the rain, paint my body, coloring books, pole/chair dancing, and many more advanced tools of the sensual arts, kept me alight.

Sometimes it's counter-intuitive to be playful when going through a divorce, launching or managing a business, paying bills, responding to creditors, working two jobs, raising children or simply being what we call "responsible" in our lives. I offer a reframe, as responsible. You have options on how you respond. We simply have carried our responsibility as a burden, rather than a privilege. This art of play, flirting, and seduction are central to the ability to manifest our Purpose, Pleasure, and Passion. Juicy Spirit is more than orgasm chasing and ways to keep or get a LOVER! Sometimes women enter into these zones of pleasure studies with the intent to keep their partner from straying. Unfortunately, we have a magazine title consciousness when it comes to sexuality just as much as men who love porn, such as how to give mind blowing head, squirt like porn star, the art of anal play, and so on. There is nothing wrong with any of this. It is a part of the benefits of pleasure, NOT the central deliverable in my experience. When we focus on "keeping" someone else, it is often the beginning of losing one's self. The Juicy woman transforms anything she's chasing into magnetism for her own retrieval restoration. The Journey is YOU, quenching your own thirst in any area using pleasure activations, leveraging your passion and reigniting your purpose! Let's face it. Underneath all the hiding, helping, and hoopla is a JUICY place inside of you that is beyond, "being GOOD in bed, when you can be GREAT in bed and beyond!" Choosing to expand your Pleasure, Passion and Purpose using Sensual Spiritual processes and your own body as a ministry, takes courage, consistency, and an uncommon call; it's the juiciest one of all.

Someone say that JUICY SPIRIT is a movement; I say it's a movement within *movements*! Movements that moved me. Movements that I found to be *home* to my soul. I have so many sister communities, however, I have a special name for sisters on this road with me. We even have a special language; it's called freedom. There are many women in leadership in the front of the room or on the stage and with many accomplishments that are still bondage to them. You'll never know just by looking upon what another has or her performance. Stop looking at appearances from the outside, in. This is how we begin comparing ourselves to other women. We can ask each other and share with each other, but truth isn't always pretty and packaged for display. While our deeper process is often private, we need spaces to process deeply. Bondage can't coach or counsel a woman who's tasted her freedom. The Juicy process allows you to taste, smell, feel, and hear your freedom. I was not just inspired. Inspiration doesn't last long enough before you need more of it to keep going. This is how we get burnt out and stressed about people finding out that we don't have it all together. Being Juicy, whether speaking of personal power or the sweet spot in our lives doesn't require that we have it all together. Juicy is the willingness to give yourself permission to explore why a woman feels she has to have it all together, so that you see yourself and most of all your beliefs that bound you about you, as a woman and in relation to our life events. Some beliefs about our sacred selves are fear-based and represent a very old paradigm. Yet, with each century we go through a new paradigm shift. We have forgotten so many of basics that derive from higher law. How we define ourselves by the same practices have become very external. For instance, cooking and caring for our home is central to womanhood as we know it. That has changed through time. What has not changed is that there is an alchemical presence every woman has to what she brings. If she wants to influence the chemistry of her home, then she may cook herself or if her lifestyle allows her, she can direct her staff. Her influence is chemical, no matter whether she acts like a modern-day medicine woman or an earthly herbal goddess. There are many faces of the Goddess. We have to find our own. This is the benefit of sisterhood. Every woman deserves a JUICY Sisterhood once she's awakened and committed to *live* it. It is in the presence of, what I call my Tribe of The FREE Sisterhood, that I am able to be silly, ridiculous, profane, *anointed*, student, teacher, big mama, and little girl… all at the same damn time! As yourself, if you have put on or edited yourself continuously, is it sisterhood if you don't feel safe? The answer depends on filters you are still covered by old paradigm thought patterns that no longer serve you or being in the company of those committed to clean the filter or remove them based on the new paradigm you're choosing to create for yourself.

Juicy Journal Truth:

List what you consider a guilty pleasure, then consider how you feel when you partake in it.
Where in your life would you like to have more personal power?
What excites you about the life that you crave?
What stops you from going for what you crave?
Is that belief about it serving you or something outside of you?

Chapter 4 : Pleasing God?

"When you order your priorities according to YOUR purpose (anointing) and not someone else's, you may stretch but you won't strain yourself trying to be anything other than you were created to be!" —**Taylor Made Inspirations**

We are created to be Juicy. Hydration for the woman is just as important for the spiritual experience as it is for the sensual and sexual experience. Unfortunately, fear-based, dogmatic religious rules and interpretations of "pleasing God," dehydrates the most obedient woman. Oftentimes, the obedience is confined to the context of a time in history or a culture that had a different agenda that opposes direct relationship with our spirituality. Patriarchy in the major religions dare not invite a woman to question or challenge her position at home, in her body and/or in the world abroad. Therefore, women have to choose it for themselves. We are designed with a blueprint for pleasure, to please and be pleased. The Creator designed a beautiful and brilliant system in service to all of the roles assigned to us as women. Our design offers ministry beyond "behavior." Women have a section in our anatomy exclusively designed for pleasure. Eight thousand nerve endings and neurotransmitters for the body, certainly act the same for the mind and the spirit. **Did the Creator make a mistake?** I'd say emphatically, "No!" Yet, a disconnect happened. Some have been taught it was with Eve, who is called the first woman. Historically, there is information from Biblical scholars overriding this theology. I definitely wasn't taught that there was another woman before Eve. In Jewish literature, she is known as Lilith. The one who rebelled in the garden story. My intention is to encourage those who worry about there being a conflict in pleasing God is to study and research. Do your own personal investigation of the truth. So, I ask: **Why is pleasing God (Spirit) and pleasure separate for you or any woman?** Any answer, other than, **"It's not,"** is usually fed by fear, frustration or misinformation.

I used to be that woman years ago. In fact, I did not have sex with my first husband until our wedding night because of my dedication to the tenants of my religion. I wanted God to bless me. The wedding night was funny. I got married in a purple Muslim garment, in the home of a Baton Rouge Court Appointee, and then had a reception with my family. Purple was my favorite color, even then. I was a college student on a very limited budget and was active in the mosque, where it wasn't uncommon for marriages to happen like this, as not to fornicate. While it wasn't just legal sex for me, it was a fast courtship. I only had friends from South and a couple of people from the mosque present. We went to dinner afterwards and I confess it was awkward later in the hotel room. I had used the vaginal sponge to protect me from pregnancy. I was so nervous about pregnancy, that I magically attracted an allergic reaction to the spermicide in the sponge. I had no idea what was going on and my new husband was certainly alarmed. We laughed about it later, but trust and believe that it wasn't funny that night. We had followed the good old rules and wanted to consummate our marriage, but was not rewarded. You may recall moments of following the rules and being disappointed on the other side. Did you question the rules or yourself? I questioned myself quite a bit that night, because I was embarrassed. I wondered what was wrong with me and I don't even remember if I confided in anyone to ask for support. Somehow, I figured it out. It would be the first time that my honey pot would teach me about the relationship that we had, mind, body or spirit. I confess that I was dogmatic about following rules, after being a teenager who got in so much trouble because of my response to authority. I started to "be good," so that people would love me more and by college so that God could love me. At least, that's what I was taught. When the elephant in the room of my soul was, I wanted to feel loved and the glaring truth was – I didn't feel loved. That feeling of the absence of love, acknowledgement or support drives many very early in our lives. So many of us want material things, want the intangible and don't know how to ask. Even the most accomplished woman, may find a way to get her needs met by performance or security. Eventually, the unmet needs return, after all of the accolades, and very often, in matters of the heart, conflict resolution and communication. Once I got clear and stepped outside of the boxes I inherited, I stopped living out of boxes and found how to have my power and pleasure **as** God/dess' presence. **That's Juicy and Juicy is magical in opening the closed places that we cover over.** If I had called it Ju-Ju Spirit, most of you certainly would not have any parts of it. We've already established how religious conditioning makes us reject first, as a knee jerk reaction.

Sis, you are magical, and feminine arts offer us tools to unlock our magic, and infuse our lives in our love, work, and health to receive the benefit your juicy femininity. It's the healthy juju, when you fall in love with yourself and stop being afraid of your desires or appetite, sexual or otherwise. **Ladies, I know I said this earlier but I want you to interrupt this tendency… so many of us have such a HIGH threshold for PAIN and a low threshold for PLEASURE! ENOUGH ALREADY!** So, I have a few questions. Get out a pen and paper because your answers may lead you to an "aha moment" or at least awareness of the places that you do NOT desire to go or maybe avoided.

Grab Your Journal and Explore:

When will YOU come down from the cross created by the habits, hurts and learned helplessness that has conditioned you along the journey to survive or *take one for the team*?

What new legacy would like to create beyond pain, guilt, and/or shame for your choices of your parents?

What are you *craving* beyond the veil of your image or self-protection?

Sometimes we spend our lives, *majoring* in *minor* things and I do mean "spend." Nothing makes it clearer how precious life really is than your own mortality or that of a loved one.

I mean, *really*... Those words you just spoke, are they life-giving or life-altering that honors the God in another person? I don't care what your creed is, if *love* is not on the main line then neither is Jesus, Buddha or Muhammad! If the company you hold requires you to keep secrets, harbor nothing in your heart, or isolate yourself from life, consider the mini death to your soul. Even if that company is lying next to you or the clock you punch, does it take your life or add to it?

======

The Bible is quoted as saying, "The wages of sin is death." Have you studied that outside of your tradition? I'll simplify it here: sin is not about Ten Commandments; sin is anything that will cause you to live inauthentically and separates you from love. This is important for you to investigate and verify. The very word itself was born out of a sport, pre-Constantine, much like throwing darts. So, when someone would throw the dart and miss the center it was called a sin for the scorekeeper. We do that with God. We have reduced "The God of our understanding," to be a scorekeeper. Oooh that's petty! Men reinterpret ancient teachings and reduce our relationship to that understanding as a petty one. The word "sin" was adopted and repurposed, much like everything else in all of the major religions. The greatest act of love is: TO THINE OWN-SELF BE TRUE!

Believing that you are wearing a scarlet letter is, NOT Juicy!

On my coaching days inside of our Juicy Spirit Process, I am met with private messages that no matter how open and safe the process is, a sister will share a secret she has labeled dark. You know, the dark secret that has a hold on you? I met the truth of a sister who had been diagnosed with herpes and felt stained and somewhat disabled to express her sensuality freely because of this diagnosis. It moved me so deeply to remember the scarlet letter. So many women are no longer wearing it on the outside but now wear the scarlet letter on the inside. This inbox to me was a first step to her freedom. It was like entering into the confessional. If you grew up Catholic, like I did, then you'll remember how you enter into the small box with two doors one for you and the other for the priest on the other side. Between you and the little bench was a screen so that you can talk to the priest. This particular morning, through several unplanned hours of coaching, I wrote to her and then to many other women. I researched more medical information from my favorite doctor, Dr. Christiane Northrup, who addressed this herpes issue directly as a medical lie that it's not reversible on her radio show. You see, when you show up, the healing balm shows up to greet you when you enter into your shadow or question it.

I offer this to *every woman* who has stamped "herself" with a scarlet letter! The scarlet letter energy is the secret shame that gets stored away in the vault of our womb and is covered over with perfectionism, performance, persecution and paralysis. It matters not what your verb is that turned you into a noun other than a Goddess. Be it the abortion, multiple abortions, STDs, poor choices, teen pregnancy, infertility, religious sacrifice, and/or all of the above. That was an experience! SISTER… That is not the total sum of *who* you are!

I know what society has programmed you and others to believe. I know what doctors have published. I know what the preachers said and have said. I can only imagine what your own parents and siblings may have said to you and about you, if they were ever present. *What do you say?* What investment are you willing to make to reprogram the years of lies and curses that have been spoken over your life? Your consideration of these questions is a value proposition. It is an internal stand-off with unworthiness, not being enough, not being good enough, and invisibility. For some of you it has become spiritual warfare. Life is going to keep on doing what life does, and you will have to press through conversations of time, money, and a magic wand. It is the willingness to surrender to pleasing "others" that will bring you to your abundant, loving place. You know something is special about you. Your *yoni* awaits your blessing and approval.

You are *worthy* to possess yourself. You are *worthy* to interrupt the patterns and programs that have run your life, relationships, parenting, and even your worship. Yes, I said "worship." You do not have to climb up the rough side of the mountain in order to access the life that you deserve. You are worthy to experience your sensuality, your joy, and be the light of the world. YOUR world. You are worthy to live through conscious choice and be co-creative with the essence of yourself, which is God/Goddess/Holy I AM/Force/Power/JUICE! You are worthy to be, do and have LOVE!

One way to access this is to make a choice and entertain (host) your divinity, truth, and forgiveness. Shame and guilt are terrible twins that have clones imbedded in mores of this culture. Question them! Do your own investigation of the truth and know that the answer lives in the same room as the question. You are the answer that you've been waiting for to be your own JUICY GOOD THING!

~ *Juicy Confession on Religion* ~

Let's connect a little more about the "religious-and-compliant-me" to understand more of what birthed me. Before I became the Juicy Goddess that I am, I confess: I may have even a GOD CHASER because of my love and submission to spiritual "concepts. I felt called to ministry very early in my life. Like anything else, when you feel called to a thing, you look in proximity to the world you know. I thought I'd be a nun. (First time sharing that publicly) I got all A's in religion. I grew up in a family that was both Catholic and Baptist. That was the beginning of my dual-language in spiritually. It made me flexible but the Holy Spirit and my Ancestors fed my curiosity and thirst. I've traveled through my Christianity with a shortstop in Buddhism (family wouldn't have that), then Islam, and back to a progressive Christianity, then serious metaphysics in my Coach and ministry preparation.

I was organically a bridge walker! I served in a traditional pulpit with my metaphysical credentials and taught it every chance I was up to preach. I naïvely wanted to provoke people to study in my sermon preparation and delivery. Later, I learned some valuable yet stinging lessons about the industry of church.

While I was not overly churched, I was a recovering Catholic by the time I got to Southern University and started studying Islam on the steps of T.T. Alien's Business Building. It's highly probable that my young "juicy" self had me on those steps because of how fine the men were that also lined the steps in their Greek paraphernalia. Whew, Lawd! Let's refocus. Those days are significant though. Even as I met new conversations about my beliefs on those steps, I studied the information being presented. I would take information shared by my new Jaguar friends, my Bible, a dictionary, and other sources into the library on campus and stay there for hours. It was part of my spiritual muscle.

If it's not a part of yours, it will have to be something that you adopt and nurture. Being told what to believe and what not to believe often makes us spiritually lazy. However, in order to activate our own sacred juices, we cannot put old wine in new wine skin. Patience is more juicy than rushing and being impatient with your process. While I was disciplined to study, I continued to find how much I did not know. Studying connected the dots I already had along my journey. I experienced the text and saw the codes, simply stated differently on a surface level. However, spirituality is very much connected to the Law of Nature and Science. It seemed that confirmations would come from places and the people I wasn't seeking out. Studying this way is magical, enlightening, and enlivening. I reinforced all that I had already been taught, but with the ability to know what was more of indoctrination created by a patriarchal root, which is linear, controlling, and rule bound. There is a 360° of knowledge available to us, which is circular. His is the circle or cycle of life in the Woman. For women to be reduced or be left out of sacred text as source energy, leaves not only the resource imbalanced. The masculine and the feminine is a creative force together. It lives inside of us and is often called Yin/Yang or our Chi. Chi is energy. God is energy. The energy of God is measured in Universal Law. Understanding Universal Law in the context of traditional scriptures opened me for direct revelation that I later found through more study backed by science and ancient wisdom.

Maybe you began your journey with a love for God and stopped there in what is the familiar. That's okay. In fact, I've studied the story of the Prodigal Son and I see the blessing of being "prodigal by design" versus the old way of teaching it as a curse. In between my spiritual travels, life brought me many lessons and opportunities to venture away from prescriptions for my spiritual life. In my move away from religion, I began to meet my JUICY unlimited self, expand and *reinvent* (cocoon) myself. **Prodigal is necessary and truly is Holy Boldness.** Conformity is easy. Living Juicy and spiritually is the willingness to give yourself room to take the journey even after having direct revelation. I subconsciously wanted to belong to something. Yet, I had set out on another course. At the time, I was seen as weird, bougie or just plain crazy by many of my family and friends. Some people are not able to start their journey, and that's ok. Others are quietly seeking and shedding, while maintaining appearances because too much is at stake. This is often true for those in leadership areas where other people's lives depend on them. However, it's realizing that your life depends on you, is an invitation to explore what pleasing God means to your healing. Healing doesn't have to mean that something is "wrong," either. Healing can simply be a choice to experience another aspect of yourself with an abiding self-love.

"If we could recover a sense of the holiness of eros and its creative, divine place in the nature of things, we might see how absurdly small our view of sex has been, and we might reinstate it without moralism at the center of life, where it can offer vitality and intimacy of unrivaled power. Before we can give depth and richness to our sexuality, we have to discover the value of deep pleasure and desire and at the same time relax our anxious attention to the control of the emotions, the justification of our lives by work and restraint, and our belief in the value of repression and suffering."

—Thomas Moore, The Soul of Sex

Of course, when I discovered that there is no separation of the spiritual, sensual and sexual, it spilled into my own life and made my life JUICY. You are spiritual already. Your spiritual journey includes everything that makes you Juicy. Sexuality is perhaps the most spiritual pathway one can access and ascend, when used as such. Sacred sexuality is not new, even if the term is new to you. There are so many clues in our spiritual systems about the power of our womanhood. We see it hidden in plain sight, like Easter and its connection with both the Spring Equinox and the Resurrection. The woman is the Holy Grail (highly sought after) and acts as a sacred chalice that the world takes its drink. When

"Mama ain't happy, nobody's happy" is found to be true whether referring to Mother Nature or our own households. Our world depends on women more than it seems, at times. We influence our homes, the way that we do business and influence the culture. Satisfied women in mind, body and spirit create a juicy world of satisfied girls, who keep birthing and loving families with their juicy magic. It can be you, should you do your work. Juicy simply requests that you play, also. Play fully in pleasing your Holy, I am, where there is no separation. We see movements happening in women all over the world, where women are reclaiming their voice and ending the pattern of suffering in silence.

The truth is, it always has in private and safe circles, after matriarch cultures simply embodied Goddess wisdom they were lynched or imprisoned. The formation of The Early Church made these wisdom circles illegal not because of sanctity or purity but simply because it was about control. It is difficult to control tribes of women who were in possession of themselves and their Divine Nature. These women often do not bow. While attempts were made to obliterate families, who lived in sacred awareness went underground, small circles migrated and preserved this knowledge and made them their own, such as with The Sexual Teachings of The White Tigress or Geisha societies. Some writings call her The Courtesan, The Seductress or Sacred Prostitute. These studies offer major clues, but the roadmap is within each woman. There are always many more sources. I found my home in myself here. It is my prayer that those who take this journey will find theirs as well.

> *"Female sexual pleasure, rightly understood, is not just about sexuality, or just about pleasure. It serves, also, as a medium of female self-knowledge and hopefulness; female creativity and courage; female focus and initiative; female bliss and transcendence; and as medium of a sensibility that feels very much like freedom. To understand the vagina properly is to realize that it is not only coextensive with the female brain, but is also, essentially, part of the female soul."* —Naomi Wolf, ***Vagina, a New Biography***

Perhaps I carried a past life experience that fed my own fear of teaching this truth of sensual spirituality. I refer to the Ancestors because that's who I called on when I was at a lost with my trust for humans and my own process. In my prayer time, I called on the mothers of my lineage to assist in *healing* myself and my womb. The mother wound offers a deep, cellular level of healing. Many women are not given permission to openly speak about it because "mothers" are often taboo to discuss. It was my womb and embrace of my sensual and sacred desires to be a mother that organically order my steps to the right book, the perfect teacher(s) and appreciation for the ones I'd already had in front of me. You see, when a woman has been or felt unmothered or under-nurtured, it is difficult to receive "mothering" from others even if they are right there to give it. This awareness was the first step of many healing cycles for me and my clients. My steps were ordered from there. The student (me) was ready and the teaching and teachers appeared one after another, male and female. All were in sacred circles of process, initiation and activation of the essence of ancient spiritual truths related to womanhood that have been concealed. I believe every woman senses this truth exists, even if she resists it. I did. After all, I embodied the sensuality, engaged the spirituality, yet I complied with leading sentiment of virtuousness.

JUICY JOURNAL EXPLORATION:

Note: Build on the questions provided in the middle of the chapter.
In what ways have you considered yourself "damaged goods," if at all?
What did you have to study or explore outside of what you've been taught about your current understanding of God and God in you, as you and through you?
What beliefs about your love, sex or month have you intentionally recreated after new understanding?

Chapter 5 : Not Juicy!

"When you continually, sacrifice yourself for others. You make THEM A THIEF." —***A Course In Miracles***

When a woman is Overwhelmed, Overextended, and Over It… that's NOT Juicy!

Stress is a large factor in not being able to experience orgasm. Even our children are more stressed out than we were, yet stress is stress, even later in life. Unfortunately, stress has become a normal way of being in a modern society. When a woman is stressed, she is often unable to relax, allow and receive *from* her senses being turned on. Rushing from one task to the next and constantly multi-tasking and saving everyone creates a ripple effect of all things, NOT JUICY! All of you who are OVERwhelmed, OVERextended and OVER It need to be hydrated by your juices as a radical act of mental health, but often you'll tell yourself you don't have time to luxuriate, create healthy boundaries or just slow down and take a nap. Naps are juicy. A well-rested woman is juicy. I understand life happens and happens *fast* and it doesn't start out being our intention to live in survival mode or even overdrive. Being turned on and attuned to your juiciness does not exempt life from happening to you or to me. We have habits that we've been holding, oftentimes a minimum of 30 years for the women that I coach. I've heard this from at least three women a week sometimes, while activating their juices. "This process is stretching me outside of my comfort zone." What comfort zone? The one that has you on a job that you hate for another year, making less than you deserve? The toxic end of a relationship that has left you depleted and disillusioned? The sexual frustration of desiring one thing but continuously getting less than you deserve? The health crisis that your body is speaking because you've been unwilling to speak for it? Tell me, which comfort zone? You are masterful enough to *be here* to respond to the call inside yourself that ENOUGH IS ENOUGH!

If the comfort zone is working, and if you like, then I love it. If not, *why* would you bury in the discomfort? It is because being overwhelmed, uncomfortable, scattered, guarded, and in survival mode has become normal? That normal will live until you funeralize it, instead of having it bury you! When the idea that *pleasure* can be the springboard for every decision you make, everything that you attract and everything that you desire to *shift*, becomes foreign! Pleasure is a healing process that interrupts the pain-body. Pleasure is a power to process beyond the normal of pain, performance and pressure. The performance anxiety is recycled when you avoid telling your story, investing in a *new normal* with your presence and possession of your precious self. *You are your own Juicy Precious Thing.*

Your shadow is not the total sum of you. The expiration date on your marriage is not a statement of passing of failure. The STD is not the final word on your womanhood and who will want to stimulate your juices. The diagnosis is not a betrayal of your body or your own self-betrayal or the registration you chose for that season. *Declare yourself unstuck, Sister! Unmask yourself* and know that love is present in your presence. No one will know that you're burning the candle at both ends, until you make it known.

You don't have to have all the answers in order to engage your senses, sensibilities and sensuality. The *Juicy Spirit is not school*, but you are unschooling yourself and updating your files! Look at the point you yielded to the expectations of everything except your own. Those areas, no matter how noble, spiritual or inspired, can be sticking points to hide and play it safe. Your Juicy Spirit calls you into *the game* of your sacred womanhood, feminine beauty, and the seduction of Universal Law that cares not about your story but is activated by your *desire*, *presence* and *commitment*. Lay down the masks that keep you in survival, cover-up, and defense mode, ready to strike. You must be tired, irritable, missing in action and *distracted*. How you operate is often grounded in how you've conditioned yourself to do everything. Come OUT sister! Press into your pleasure exploration with a curious mind and know your story is not up to a judge and jury. Your story is not meant to hide you, it's meant to heal you, awaken your senses, and possess the essence of your own JUICE! What masks are you willing to lay down? ONE WORD!

Some of the answers that I received from the sisterhood were:

1. Perfectionism
2. Control
3. Acceptance
4. Knowing
5. Self-sufficiency
6. People pleasing
7. Fear
8. Displeasure
9. Anger
10. Conformity
11. Settling
12. Lack

What are you afraid someone will see about you beyond the veil?

Here is an example of my coaching to a Juicy Butterfly Goddess, who took her mask off and told the truth about "the overs," mentioned earlier. I saw this opening for her and told her these words: *I am cheering you. I am willing to coach you on this spiritually erotic journey. You are aching for it and so is your husband. Now, watch your income soar and requests for more business. Watch the children get happier. Let them see their parents smooch and eventually tell them why you all need TIME and a ZONE. Yes! Not enough black families have SEEN the love and affection of a unit they are IMPRINTED with. You have that chance now. LET YOUR FREAK FLAG FLY, BAEBAY!!!!! Twerk somethin, werk something!*

This Juicy Butterfly mother and wife experienced all over the "overs" and used pleasure-purpose-passion to take her higher. I gave her some coaching and tools to use and apply in her first acknowledgement of "the overs." She accepted the stretches I offered and returned with results that shifted the situation. Her follow-up after creating some space to make requests, set some boundaries, tell her truth, and speak her desires to her husband:

Wow Sisters....I don't even know where to begin. Where do I rejoin the conversation? You Juicy women have been at it from what I can see! Ain't no party like a Juicy Butterfly party....and the Juicy Butterflies don't stop! Lol It's been a minute since my last post. I've been on hiatus since my Destin getaway. All I can say is, it was an incredible TANTRIC experience that kept me on high from the moment of arrival to the moment of ARRIVAL! (wink, wink). I shared with you all about how I felt my job was "draining" me of energy... well before and after (surprisingly not so much during) my vacation, I was feeling completely exhausted even after resting. I decided to do a cleanse/fast and unfortunately that made things even worse. Turns out I was robbing my body of necessary iron nutrients on top of already being severely anemic (which was also a surprise). This my dear sisters landed me in the hospital for a few days where I underwent a blood transfusion, impending iron IV therapy, and of course aggressive testing to determine the cause. As you can imagine with 3 young children underfoot, I've needed to simply take a minute to just be.

I needed to get my mind right and have been truly applying the lessons learned here and through other natural health and healing sources, and what I can say for sure is that through it all… even on that hospital bed, I have remained juicy (even if only in my head) and the world continues to respond. Every experience I have these days I see the blessing, I feel the bliss, I am served and experiencing love in action. I mean everyone from the doctors to the dang on food service person has accommodated me in such a way that I've felt nothing but joy, gratitude and pleasure. One might ask, how is it possible to experience pleasure in a hospital bed or while on bed rest? A few months ago, I would have been asking that question too. But not today… I get it La Tonia Taylor. What you have done for me, my marriage, my family is simply DIVINE! I can't put a price on it, but the joy I feel… honey that investment has yielded a multitude of blessings. How does the song go… "The joy I feel the world didn't give it and the world can't take it away…" Baabay…that's my living mantra today. The only way I can explain it is to say that my mind is different and every experience I have conforms to that reality. And, Rev Coach La Tonia you were spot on about the children being happier and more cooperative (praises for that cuz that 2-year-old has the willpower) and the business… well we just received a contract from David's Bridal corporate to do some work on their fall catalog – BIG! And…if I can just testify… Brides are calling us DAILY from everywhere (including Los Angeles) and booking over the phone. Typically, the level of grind and hustle that would be needed to produce the volume of calls we are getting would be exhausting. But today FAVOR Reigns! And my womb is quivering with excitement. Funny thing….as soon as I stepped out of some else's dream to build my own, the heavens just opened up to pour us out blessings!

I was so happy to hear from this Juicy Butterfly. Big Mama Juicy, over here, had to practice trust and surrender of the Goddess in her and allow her drifts in and out to be exactly the pattern she came to face. This sister was no stranger to a coaching process; she knew how to process herself into the analysis of paralysis. We do that well in certain coaching communities, but what I have learned and offer is *surrender* of the process and the need for perfection. I explained to her how fasting, when you are you malnourished on ANY way is unloving and self-sabotage. Women in the process of becoming juicy are choosing to activate a season of HYDRATING! Hydrate yourself with yourself, your desires and the *divine surprises* that feed them. I was so humbled by her stretch and her evidence of using her voice, her power center. There is more! We must have the courage to speak our desires into the atmosphere, even if it's to tell on ourselves or put others on notice. There is always more when coming from a place of abundance, not lack and scarcity. You know that you are being authentic and speaking from the voice of your feminine pulchritude when the environment in and around you shifts. Sometimes, this is all that is needed when experiencing a healing crisis. Confessing that you can see yourself, what you're doing or have been doing and what you are willing to change immediately. Then, do it! Do it from a juicy mind that understands pleasurable, orgasmic and self-loving living is a priority that cannot be starved by being a mother, wife, friend or sister and superwoman to others without first saving yourself. What message is your body giving you today? No matter your answer, I *give thanks*!

You see sister, when you *speak*, you set not only yourself free… you set another woman free. A big sister also helped me to see and lovingly called me out on the disservice I do when I hold back from the space. I had been told this before in leadership training by a mentor. In one of our training sessions, I was holding my gift of clairsentience and clairvoyance to the point where it made me physically ill. I didn't even know that I was doing it. Let me explain how deep this nudge was for me. As a child I often got in trouble for my mouth. I challenged authority at times I should not have, I'm sure. It began the moment I felt I couldn't trust adults to protect me from many things, molestation was one of them. However, my mother said things to me in anger that hurt deeply. I was a walking wounded child, especially after my parents' divorce. My heart was broken, too. No one seemed to know this at the time, nor was therapy popular or all of this evolved language we use today. I learned how to hold my tongue in order to *not* get in trouble or lose love. My mentors and loving sisters never let me settle into this story. So, this is another reason why it's good to orbit with those who keep you rotating in the direction of continual growth and expansion. There are some shifts that cannot be read in a book, Googled or found on social media. As women, there are only some experiences that are learned in community, in process and in journeying together.

Most of you are and have always been a sensual *Goddess*. You look like you could teach the session. *Own it!* Breath it. Stand in it. Allow it to continue to heal and transform you every day of your life. It will not make you exempt from life doing what life does. That's a magic pill and the only pill there is *awakening* or *sleep*. You chose to awaken. There is more. More of you that you have not met yet. More of life that you will desire to taste, feel, smell and feel. More of God (Divinity) in it all. What has been profane will become sacred because your eyes can see. Can you sense that? There are women waiting on you but *you go first!* No rush to regurgitate, just become. People come to you because you are beautiful! *Inside* and *out*!

Chapter 6 :
PLEASURABLY PREGNANT
(Juice Your Bliss)

"Follow your bliss. If you do follow your bliss, you put yourself on a kind of track that has been there all the while waiting for you, and the life you ought to be living is the one you are living. When you can see that, you begin to meet people who are in the field of your bliss, and they open the doors to you. I say, follow your bliss and don't be afraid, and doors will open where you didn't know they were going to be. If you follow your bliss, doors will open for you that wouldn't have opened for anyone else."
—Joseph Campbell, Author & Mystic

After my womb spoke, I eventually had a myomectomy, the surgical removal of fibroids. They were small but painful during ovulation because of their positioning in the uterine wall and one right at the vaginal opening. That may be too much information but I share it because not everyone needs surgery and had I known or paid more attention to what I already knew, I would have taken a different route. I was tired of the pain and I thought I wanted to get pregnant with my second husband. Only after the fibroids were removed, did my womb reveal more. We were having a better relationship, now. I was present with her and she was present with me. I did my work in therapy, on massage tables, underneath Reiki hands, herbal therapy, and de-stressing my life. When I went to my naturopath, an integrative medical doctor, for post-op examination, she gave me a total evaluation, like I'd never experienced in my life. The one thing that she said, after I told her that I was certain that did not want to conceive with this man, even now that I can. She said to me, "My prescription is that you get pregnant with yourself. Take nine months and follow this regimen." I did, however, I included an immersion into a pleasure-centered process. Pleasure allowed me to get pregnant with myself. Pleasurably pregnant with purpose… much like sex, is not limited to the physical nor is pregnancy.

So many of you are *pregnant* and carrying a vision that has yet to be birthed. When I do "this" work, I continue to be born again in spiritual understanding of how unlimited feminine practice begins with pleasure is a woman's transformation. Our work, not my work because we are not alone, once we begin. We are supported by a legacy of women who carried vision in their own wombs, some birth and some aborted by many conditions beyond their control. Either way, a woman who is pleasurably pregnant connects to her purpose. Your mental, emotional and spiritual womb must expand. Even the concept of birth is just as limited as is the concept of sensuality or orgasm. Sensuality, orgasm and pleasure are not always the same thing but each offers medicine for rebirth, soul revival, and reinvention. And guess what? Check the stats: Your very *life force* depends on it! There are certain eyes that can see your fullness, even when you try to cover it up or are distracted by all that you *do*. Oh, this pregnancy is *immaculate* and will get your attention. I see you carrying your lode and I appeal to you, let's birth this or these babies, which are your desires, and your vision! You must *make* room to continuously give birth to YOU.

We limit so many creative impulses to be one dimensional, when everything about sensuality-sexuality is multi-dimensional. Copulation, procreation, pregnancy, and birth are not limited to the body. It is a mind, body, and spirit experience available to us at various levels of being.

So many of us on the *Womanhood* journey have become conditioned to have a *high pain threshold* and *low joy* Limit. What if your cup can run over with *joy juice* just waiting on permission (from you) to be activated? Consider your deepest most passionate desires. Pleasure in never a threat, unless it's been disabled by guilt or shame nor is pleasure limited to our genitals. Pleasure is a doorway that leads to the conception of more desire for the good life that you deserve. Pleasure is a ministry that whispers directly into your ear about your divinity and worthiness. Pleasure is a healer, not an escape hatch. Pleasure demands radical self-care, tender affection, self-definition, delightful understanding of your own preferences and erogenous zones. Pleasure increases your vibrations to discipline yourself through small acts of service as a signal to your birthright for simplicity and luxury. Yes, pleasure occupies the divine dichotomy of all things. This is Universal Law integrated via the Pleasure Principle. What you seek is seeking you.

This pregnancy allows you access expectation for more pleasure and leverage it to become magnetic, rather than always in labor and never birthing your heartfelt desire. Sister, to be pleasurably pregnant with purpose begins with your five senses and extends beyond them. What evokes your bliss? You are not allowed to be basic. You know what the basics are right? Getting your hair and nails done are the basics. Eating healthy are the basics. Dressing in clothes that fit and compliment you are the basics. Knowing your bra size and favorite colors are the basics. Going out to dinner and retail therapy are the basics. Anyone can do the basics! The mere fact that you reading this tells me that being basic is, *not you*! Sometimes we slip and fall by doing the basics because life happens. I know, because I do it. Accept this as a gentle reminder to return to the basics but don't stay there. *Bliss* is calling to you.

Bliss seduces the things we desire to us and penetrates our mind, body and spirit. Without trying, we find out just how fertile we are. When I was pleasurably pregnant, my creativity flowed. When I became pleasurably pregnant with myself, I didn't need permission to say yes to invitations that made me nervous or was out of my comfort zone. Each yes, increased my ability to choose well. When I am pleasurably pregnant and in purpose, I teach better and intimacy is effortless in my relationships. When I am pleasurably pregnant and full, I have cravings that rise inside of me for experiences that I had denied myself the missed opportunities to explore because I was too busy or too distracted. Oh yes! Pleasure is potent!

Since life has become a journey of bliss, a bliss-filled, lavish, abundance of my good and the good of others, I get pregnant with myself often. Those fibroids represented aborted visions, internalized anger and frustrated creativity. I vowed to myself play fully and follow my bliss or juice it. I honestly believe that I may have had children earlier, traveled more and had better relationships with men and money, had I known what I know now. However, I have no regrets. I know that a part of my ministerial assignment is to mother women who have been unmothered or called to understand the Cosmic Mother's activity in their life. The Universe is continuing to nudge me as I choose *bliss, joy, and orgasmic living* as a birthright. It may have always been here but I could easily have been more conformed to the examples before me who took the rough side of the mountain, often not by choice but by force. I never knew how afraid we are of the idea of bliss, pleasure, passion, and purpose, until I took on my own pleasure immersion. I meet my former self in the stories I hear in other women. We get stuck in "the story" and become impotent or disabled by the stagnation or cover-up. Somehow subconsciously, there is cognitive dissonance that has become a normal way of being for many modern women who have become disconnected from the ways of ancient feminine practices that have been hidden in plain sight. It causes us to be impotent. Sometimes answering the call is really a return to force and a power that you may have known in other lifetimes. It will feel counterintuitive to live in this place. Many women come to it like it's another "thing to do" or like a "school assignment," but no one is grading you, except you. *Trust the process* of doors opening where you wouldn't have known there were any, mostly in yourself. It is where the Divine lives, moves, and has his/her being!

~ STAYing Juicy & Working Your Process

Rites of passage processes are becoming extinct in The West, and it is foreign to adult women on how to work their process. Rites of passage are known to be for a young woman or man who is entering puberty and is celebrated with various activities that lead up to a celebration. That is the modern version. However, many rites of passage processes of old were led by elders into an unknown location or weeks of activities that fed confidence and clarity about one's ability. It is the missing link for our teens today, because we didn't have it. We became possessive about "our business" and our children. Secrets were born through our focus on earning a living and proving that we could make it on our own. This is anti-family and maturity. We are interdependent people who thrive in Divine collaboration beyond survival skills. While Juicy Spirit is a rites process that is traveled by sisters who unlock the gates of their spiritual and succulent self, women have had many natural uncelebrated crossroads that mark a transition from one way of being to another. Menstruation, intercourse, falling in love, marriage, divorce, labor and delivery, and menopause are all rites of passage that have become spiritual bypasses and missed opportunities to mother one another, sister one another and acknowledge the Divinity in womanhood. This is sensuality and the honor of our rebirth and reemergence in different forms. Yes, we deserve to celebrate our shedding, releasing, receiving, birthing, and the cycles, even every 30 days. The four seasons are within us, indicating how we get to respond to our feminine garden. The ushers, guardians, and medicine women are our escorts. Our mothers forgot, by design, and fear of the Divine Feminine.

The matriarch had her own lessons to learn in the collective experience of being a woman, and to be defined by patriarchy is actually to be confined. Patriarchy is not limited to the misuse of male power; it is the complicit participation in the distortions and attacks divinity, even if it's a female. The Divine Masculine and the Divine Feminine are seated together in the pantheon of ascended self-mastery that we call by many names, from The Saints to Orishas, Angels, Archangels, and the Disciples of various traditions. They all have a vibration that lives within the womb of a woman.

When women honor other women in this way, it will be more difficult to hold another woman in low regard or the ones that hold themselves will raise their vibration beyond the one they know. Even the ones who have come to the gateways can grow beyond our human base level experience rather than have glimpses of it. In other words, we are a sisterhood of remembering this alchemy inside of us.

Chapter 7 : Juicy Sacred Sisterhood

"I will not die an unlived life. I will not live in fear of falling or catching fire. I choose to inhabit my days, to allow my living to open to me, to make me less afraid, more accessible; to loosen my heart until it becomes a wing, a torch, a promise. I choose to risk my significance, to live so that which came to me as a seed goes to the next blossom and that which came to me as a blossom, goes on as fruit." —**Dawna Markova**

"The butterfly does not eat plants, it drinks nectar, reproduces, and soars above the garden. The butterfly has undergone a spiritual evolution as well as a physical metamorphosis." —**Excerpt from Sataya Center of Meditation**

Showing up for ourselves begins with our individual desire for pleasure or healing, but when a woman heals, she heals seven generations forward and seven generations behind her. This is no ordinary journey that I speak of, once we move through the gateway of pleasure and sensuality. Our celebration of ourselves makes room for the celebration of other women. Here is what I share with my clients who are coming out of the wilderness of womanhood and I share this with you if you have not trusted women or been hurt by women:

"You do not have to walk alone. When I accepted invitations to share and to do the work, I had to show up without giving a damn about my image. Isolation is killing us or robbing us of our life force. Too many women are on the edge of a breakdown, being lost to suicide or living and moving about totally numb. The idea that I don't want anyone in my business is born of shame and or the other extreme – arrogance. An arrogant woman is hard to reach but a woman fearful of being judged is even more difficult. It's an illusion. The illusions are created by the first set of lies told to us about whom we are, what we need to be, and what is appropriate to us to discover and share who we are. The next set of lies are the ones we tell to ourselves. The funny thing about the first set of lies is that we accept them as truth. Information accepted as truth without investigation is only *belief*. Beliefs are the absence of knowledge and sometimes operate as a spell cast. We wonder why we can't get out of a certain groove or pattern, then apply the same placebo over and over again. Some call it insanity. I call it an illusion because when a woman allows truth to penetrate her and become pregnant with herself, she gives birth to her unique vision.

Each Goddess represents an aspect of a woman's superpowers, in truth and in deed. There are scholars who specialize in this study beyond feminism or women's rights, such as Queen Afua, Dr. Jewel Pookrum, Dr. SuZar Epps, Dr. Christiane Northrup, Naomi Wolf, Dr. Clarissa Pinkola Estes, Audre Lorde, and many more. They are our mothers, sisters, and modern-day medicine women. Some of the authors, physicians, medicine women, and midwives that we now love to read and celebrate, lost everything then to tell this truth to women, when women could hear them and men and/or the systems they created destroyed them. This immersion into feminine magic in the presence of emancipated women-led tribes is bigger than someone, "being in your business." You have to trust yourself, enough to allow sacred sisterhood to mother you. Many of our mothers simply did not know, nor did their mothers. We activate a living DNA beyond our family tree when we return to our femininity and process. I know this happened with me the moment I decided to pursue my fertility and listen to the messages from my womb. At a time in my process, I reached my capacity in what I could do alone. Even when I chose to reach out, ask to be heard, and told the truth to set myself free, I discovered that my ego needed to be silenced. There is power in being witnessed. This is very different than just calling a girlfriend to vent or dump feelings in her lap to carry. It does require discernment because if the woman you are "just venting" with gives you unsolicited advice, most likely you'll shut down or follow prescriptions that she has not investigated. If she doesn't say much, most likely, you won't know her intention or feel heard. To witness a woman is a skill acquired by the woman who has journey in self, even if she's still traveling. In sisterhood, we witness each other in a very specific way.

As I coach the sisterhood of Juicy Spirit, I work with girls in schools and in general just watch us in our relationships. I notice there is something happening amongst women, regarding sisterhood. *We have forgotten how to love* one another, *woman to woman*, as a sister. There's a voice that says, "*I'm afraid of what she will think or say to me.*" What Spirit moved me to see is the *safety* that we desire is the *safety* we bring. Secure is a synonym of safe. Somewhere in our lives we were made insecure about ourselves, our womanhood and our ability to be safe in the presence of our reflection. Perhaps, some have never had the experience of sacred *safe* sisterhood. The contrast reflects our own shadow or light. Sure, the shadow exists but so does the light.

The culture then reinforces degrading messages about women and uses the most toxic examples of women interacting as mainstream. Shutting down, poisoning another woman with fork tongue, attack and hiding out is *not* the normal. Be the shift you want to see and choose to see into you (intimacy) or into-me-I-see what I desire. When feeding from shadow examples, causes spontaneous abortions and unnurtured lives in our sister tribes. The light is only accessible through proverbial prenatal care of our woman tribes.

Sister, even when you get a man, leverage your awakened juiciness to manifest new levels of prosperity or the attention of the apple of your eye… be careful not to forsake the sisterhood or girl time! That is the quickest way to *dry out*! The reason that your mate's (yang energy) is attracted to us is… our ability to spin in our own orbit and come back and *spill over with them*! Yes, you are your own orbit when you attend to your juices with pleasurable activities such as, rest, radical self-care, art, gourmet foods and flavors, body work, physical movement, dance, travel, growing your business, nature, and more specific practices offered in our rites of passage process, you orbit a beautiful fragrance that allows some mystery. Even if you've been together for years, when you rotate in your feminine orbit, you allow him to hunt for you and to see what in the world you are up to. Relationships get stale because we get lazy within them or we're so busy trying to control everything. The extremes serve no one. You see a man or mate is not responsible for making you orgasm in the body, but they can facilitate it. Taking your pleasure into your own hands (no pun intended) offers another access point of power that can also be shared. Whether a facilitated orgasm or a shared power to bring another into the experience. When you attach your orgasm (joy and fulfillment) to the one you love, you are subject to demagnetize yourself. When two magnets are placed together, they either repel or attract. These opposite totem poles show us that poles repel and opposite poles attract. This is an example of the yin and yang principle that exists inside of all of us, male and female. When we overuse one energy and under use the other, our attraction point for what we desire requires the opposite of what you may think logically. The feminine intelligence is available to any woman who calls forth a higher version of herself and the men who honor and love goddesses.

Be mindful, there is responsibility in the use of our feminine magic and ability to influence the outcomes that we desire using our sweet and juicy sacredness. Oftentimes, you'll see some amongst use high science to get what they want and then its *game over* for maintaining this sacred knowing. We can use our satisfaction to be of service to our family and our community. Being a Goddess is a lifetime journey and this is why it is important to surround yourself with women who *live their pleasure*! Once you do this, it's difficult to be around those who are parched. You may repel some of your acquaintances who are committed to war with men, being angry and rigid or even "inappropriate." There is refinement and dignity in a woman who does not apologize for laughter, her curves, and the authentic expression of herself.

Staying the course is not easy in a world were conformity is easy and non-conformity comes with fear. It is work to remember who you are, even after you've engaged your juices! Old habits die hard however commit to RE-member (bring together) all of your juice and the "new" tools you have. You cannot love yourself and hate other women; spirit is not in that nor is it juicy. Our culture then reinforces degrading messages about women and uses the most toxic examples of women interacting as mainstream.

Women share a magic that is activated in the presence of other awakened women, otherwise we perpetuate our fear or the inheritance of fear and judgment for other women. Here are some of the wisdom from your sisters who participated in Juicy Spirit when asked about their experience with sisterhood. Here are their responses to, **"Do you trust women?"**

<u>**Deserie Johnson**</u>: Now I do. It took years for me to trust other women, to let them into my circle beyond the wall I had built to keep them out. I have had some bad experiences with women… I also wasn't always the best woman friend operating strongly in the yang with an added "don't give a fuck" attitude. When a sistah friend spoke truth to me and proceeds to show me by example what a true friend was… I not only learned to trust other women, I learned to trust myself and my ability to be a friend as well as accept my need for such bonds.

Renee Goss: For as long as I could remember I've always trusted women/sisterhood. I trusted my mother. My mom had special women in her life that she held dear. I've never seen them disrespect each other, gossip, or betray each other. It wasn't until I got older that I was exposed to the "I don't trust women" notion. It wasn't my experience but I am sensitive to women who struggled in the area of trust.

Monique Michele Sadler: I have always trusted women "in spite" of messages I received from my mother. My mom has never had a lot of women friends and OMG would NEVER join a women's group. Meanwhile, I was always the opposite, having lots of girlfriends and becoming a member of a sorority (Skee Wee ;-) Love that the heart chakra is pink and green. In general, she is cautious of people's motives – especially women. When it comes to women/girls, I remember growing up with messages like, "Tell so much and keep so much," "Mmph, there's something about THAT one," "She's jealous of you deep down," or "Watch her." Just the other day, I was talking with my mother about two former girlfriends I reached out to recently in the spirit of forgiveness and concern. Not because I wanted to rekindle the relationships with either one of them, but because things were going on their lives that I wanted to acknowledge and show heartfelt prayer and concern for. Neither one of these women returned my call/text and totally ignored my outreach, which was really fine with me. My mother nearly blew a gasket, "Why would you do that?" I told her because I wanted to let them know that I was thinking of them, regardless of the status of our relationship. I didn't care what they "thought" about it. She said that the thing she regrets most about friendships that have ended is feeling like she wasted time with women who didn't deserve it. I told her, that I don't feel that way about either of these women. While we are no longer friends, I value and hold the scared time we were friends and by reaching out in forgiveness set myself free. It doesn't matter what their response was or wasn't. I think my mother is in awe of my attitude at times, but worries for me at the same time. She is 73-years-old and I see the results of her not having close relationships with women. I think she would have more balance in her life if she did. I try and work with her, but she is set in her ways. I've been blessed to have some great relationships with women in my inner circle (and even outside of it) and in spite of a few disappointments, I so value sisterhood and love learning more about and connecting with my feminine power.

Dr. J: For the past few months I have been experiencing encounters with women and sisters to let me know I need to slow down and pay attention. As La Tonia spoke last night, it CONFIRMED where I am… Many times, as women, we tend to seek out and trust those sisters who reinforce our less enlightened root beliefs. I'm not a spokesperson, so I will say, "I have done that," in the recent past. It wasn't until early January after my surgery that I slowed down enough to recognize those sisters I was holding close were the very ones who reinforced me going in circles. In fact, they cheered as I ran faster and faster in the same dysfunctional circle. I would subliminally push the *enlightened* sisters further outside of the circle based on comments the inner circle sisters shared. You may have heard these comments before:

Girl, I wouldn't listen to her… She probably likes your husband/man…

We have known you forever! They just met you. They don't understand you like we do.

You should take that deal. It sounds like a no-brainer (knowing it's outside of your highlighted path).

The whole scene looked pretty much like the scene in *The Wiz*, when the crows were reinforcing those negative beliefs to the Scarecrow. If you noticed in the movie, the scarecrow was never tethered to the pole, his negative thoughts kept him tied to that place.

Anyhow, I'm saying all of that to say: My current evolution has showed me *which sisters* to *trust* and which ones to leave in the field. So many times, women are afraid that *brothers* are going to be the ones who abuse their hearts, that we carelessly release our hearts to unenlightened sisters who do more damage. This module for me started with allowing my *enlightened sisters* more access to the deep places in my heart.

"No matter how "bad" or "flawed" you think you are, borrow the belief in your good from the company you keep." —<u>**Taylor Made Inspirations**</u>

Chapter 8 : Living In The Juicy Stream?

"Powerless women are women who use the masculine force to try to make everything right, constantly giving to make sure everyone is OK, overworked, tired, unfulfilled, lacking sex appeal and magnetism. Surrendered women are just the opposite." —Kenya K. Stevens

What does this mean to you?

"When you live in this stream, you live according to your heart's desires, your innermost urging and true calling, following your inner voice and listening to your natural rhythms as they harmonize with the earth, your loved ones, the cycles of time and rhythm, and life itself. The life spark within all of us, birthed from the womb, pushes toward this movement, the very movement of creativity, joy, and free sexual energy. These movements constantly go through you and the earth and are made conscious when your emotional state is agile and you can easily emote, for emotions equals energy in motion.
To align to the movements of the womb requires that you become fluid. When you are fully fluid, you can experience any feeling whatsoever at any time, at will. Thus, if you can, at will, feel delight, feel love, anger, or tears without

attachment to them, then you can be moved by Spirit, which is always fluid and open. However, the less you can summon feelings, the more you are frightened of them, the more you are at their mercy. Conversely, the more you allow yourself to experience feelings, the less you can be enslaved by them. If you allow them to pass through you, you become transparent, without holding on to anything or anybody."
—Padma Aon Prakasha, ***Womb Wisdom***

YOU ARE HERE for a reason, as woman!

Let's recap:

Juicy is the woman who feeds her vision from her overflow!

Juicy is the woman who speaks the language of desire without consulting her limits.

Juicy is the woman who figures it IN, not out.

Juicy is the woman who uses her emotional guidance system to move deeper into self-awareness and co-creation.

Juicy is led by pleasure first and allows it heal her.

Juicy is the woman who ends the conflict with her God given right to be fully expressed!

Juicy is the woman who finds God in herself and uses her discovery to water her Love, Sex and Money relationships and manifestations.

Juicy is the woman who is released from all of the shame and old stories attached to her womanly choices.

Juicy is the woman who stands in her sensual, sexual spiritual authority and heals the division of it in her that caused it to be separate.

Juicy is the woman who rehydrates herself and spills over to revive her relationships.

Juicy is the woman who commits to stewardship in sisterhood, knowing, "I am not my sister's keeper, I am she," meaning that if I see it in her it exists somewhere it me, depending what lens I'm using for sisterhood.

Let me tell you how I know my spirit awakened my feminine to become juicy and how the stream rebirths a life that is juicy. Even after all of the self-betrayals and activating my own feminine transformation through sensual awakening, I believed in love. I knew for sure that I would love again, only from a full cup that overflowed with my own turn-on and clarity about what I desired. My shadow self is less of something I deny because my rebirth required me to free myself from old wounds and the belief systems that held them in place. I no longer needed to be saved from anything by the security provided by a man.

Releasing this stream of consciousness began with denouncing traditional wedding vows, which I took in the second marriage knowing that I did not align with the energy of bondage in them. You may not agree and you don't have to. I had done the research and I love the study of words and their roots. However, the point is, I left that to assumption that the ministers knew this about me. It was the same year that my womb spoke. I knew about co-creative love as a Minister of Spiritual Consciousness. Had I forgotten? Yes, conformity will make you have amnesia even after you've been enlightened. I give thanks for facing my shadow, my ego. It reminded me of the Universal Law and its power at all times. We always get what we want at that level of consciousness. I was powerful at manifesting, even during my lack of awareness of higher law. What if I gave that same energy I'd given to my fear, to my faith in me, and my anointing? That's what I had to ask myself a few years later, with no husband as a catch-net yet a new abiding of self-love, when the nine to five ended in 2013.

That was the same year I answered with my sacred yes. It was July 3, 2013 when I took a leap of faith into my waters. I was scared as hell and holding on by a thread, except for my intent, focus, new ministry to women, and JUICY life. Little did I know it made way for me practice what I preached about riding our waves and surrendering to purpose through pleasure. I manifested an entire seven day cruise with V.I.P. accommodations, the plane ticket to get there and a layover spot with a Sister Goddess I'd never met. Prior to the trip, I was struggling to stay juicy because I had to shed my monkey-mind, also known as "employee mindset." Travel always relaxed my busy mind. Warm places nourish my feminine; this opportunity did both. While in San Diego before I boarded the ship, I performed a ritual to release old heartbreaks to make room for love. If that trip was enough to confirm this feminine magic, I returned to meet my Twin Flame while not looking. He caught me by surprise. I was juicy on the inside in such a satisfying way. That was different than two marriages prior. The voice of clarity, the same voice of direction I had been given in New Orleans on the bridge, spoke through a man from New Orleans. I had returned a day earlier than planned from my Soul Train Cruise to Mexico. Normally, I would spend Sunday cheering The New Orleans Saints with a lively crew from the bayou regions and have a good time. I thought I'd missed the game but it was a late game and I had time to get there. Something brought us together. There we were standing outside talking and I was half listening, until I heard the voice of a healed man on a spiritual journey. I didn't expect it but I knew what I heard and our conversation on that level had not stopped. We declared ourselves to one another later that night, breaking my normal rules of engagement. Nothing about our love would be normal and that matched the vows I had forgotten to insure were present. The benefits of being in my own juicy stream attracted another being in his own. Together, we have pushed the edges of the lessons we need to learn and breakthrough individually and together. My stream does not need to possess his or be possessed. Our love is a powerful, conscious choice. Spiritual choice is our vow. The moment our choice becomes bondage, or lacks growth, then we have the right to make new choices that honor the Divine that brought us together.

I had given myself three years prior to be present with my womanhood, not seeking a relationship, without the weight of timelines and guarantees from men to give me anything that I was available to access in myself. That ritual was a heartfelt signal that I was ready to love. Choosing to follow my bliss has cracked me open to be vulnerable in a way that I'd never known. We didn't fall in love or hook up. We had already known each other in other lifetimes. This connection is ancient, yet not without resistance or deeper healing required at times. However, it's welcomed. With every bold yes that I say to myself, my exploration and my own rebirth has ushered me to whole and bold choices. Challenging myself in the places that I normally put on the brakes or used intellectualize logic, cleverly disguised as core beliefs that no longer serves my evolution, was born from streaming a conscious love like this. Through growing in love with my feminine, I have grown in love with the Masculine. I believe a juicy woman heals her family line from years of battles between the masculine and the feminine, if she is a willing vessel. Even if our choices would move us to different journeys, I am expanded because I've chosen well. In the past, I chose at my level of conscious awareness. *A Course In Miracles* says, "There is nothing to heal, only more God to be revealed." My JUICY continues to reveal me and my higher choices, as each feminine lesson, desire, fulfilled desires and ways of being. I'm not perfect and both my shadow and light self invite me to interrupt the need to be much gentler with myself. The stream has lead me to deeper waters, even in my Ancestral Communication. All of this spills over into my business, my vision and my provision. My soul is watered and my life is orgasmic when I choose it to be. Juicy has opened me and the women who experience the guided process to orgasmic living.

The stream may begin with a trickle, but as you open your valves – sensually and spiritually – the stream is guaranteed. STAND IN YOUR POWER! Stand in your stream.

I called this stream Orgasmic Abundance. Along my own juicy journey and facilitating others' journey, I have often witnessed our streams being cut off by lack, worry, and anxiety about money and survival on our jobs or in our purpose. Women have been taught to separate the soft feminine from the fierce power and force that is often reserved for the boardroom or business. Therefore, with the patriarchal influence in corporate cultures breeds fear and the need to protect the mixing of business and pleasure for women in business or leadership. This is because we have an external reference point of how that looks. I teach women how to activate their stream to flow and open for their benefit and productivity at work and at large in a way that creates more abundance, as a result of their orgasmic intelligence. In 2015, I hosted a tele-summit with other practitioners who have inspired women to live "integrated" from the womb, called The Orgasmic Abundant Woman, to introduce a more *feminine business model* to open both the stream of consciousness and to connect the dots, where regimented business as usual has disconnected them for us, especially melanin rich women. We haven't trusted our stream enough to relax beyond performance measures, ratings, and competition. So, we grind, like men have modeled and it exhausts our adrenals and breaks down our capacity to trust that there will be a seat at the table of success. Orgasmic living begins with an authentic knowing of how to access the feminine without judgment that it is weak or easily manipulated. Activating feminine intelligence requires retraining the brain to remember ways to be *juicy* and live juicy, while playing the game of life with others.

Fake positivity, love, and light or martyrdom is not required. Sometimes our journey will be colorful and light, like the butterfly or grungy and low like the cocoon. Either way, we get to rebirth. Happy positive thoughts are not enough and never have been, because positive thoughts are not something we can always permanently maintain and the pressure to do that can lead to a crash. It is more about a full body being fully immersed into a lifestyle, soul orientation, commitment, devotion or core values that honor all that is sacred and a focus that has everything to do with a proactive approach to tackling the assaults and crises we are up against. This would include things like living in one's highest integrity, sharing important information, clearing one's programming that undermines our potential and distort the true nature of the masculine and feminine, and ridding ourselves from being influenced by anything that is trying to control and harm us. We have the power to evict anything we don't want.

When we stand in our power as co-creators, dreamers, activators, alchemists, facilitators, divine embodiments or catalysts to ours or someone else's healing and awakening process, without force, coercion or manipulation, there is only a choice that remains. At that point, it is not our burden to carry what people choose to do with the resources that are available to them, resources that they are only being reminded of. Our deepest purpose is to reveal the pristine template of Divine Union and our sovereign free-will that we all have access to, that is just waiting to be revealed, exposed, and be fully illuminated, honored and empowered, so that reality can begin to shift in accordance with the *truth* of who we are, rather than what we have been conditioned to be. Creation is waiting for all of us to take this stand.

You will hear me say through the journey, KEEP GOING! My motivation for the freedom ride that you are taking is Mama Harriet Tubman. Our Juicy Journey is unique and responsive to where you are in your season. Kind of like the *fruit* discussed early on! There are so many things to cause us to miss the *ripe* picking time. Some of these are the messages of our households, models of our caregivers and the mess in dogma/the ...dogmatic. Many proclaim *freedom* after being *set free* in this underground process. Own this space that you are in as Sacred and Safe! Share where women have committed to their JUICY. Keep thy own counsel with others who don't even know that they may be dry, dehydrated, and bitter. They will notice something stirring in you. Just BE IT! Freedom is a process with many layers, as many of you are along the way in different phases. Even those who are free… forget. The juicy journey is also intended to call together (re-member) the scattered pieces so that you can apply your WHOLENESS to your heart's desires. KEEP GOING!

There is a lot going on in the atmosphere and specifically in your world, and let me tell you something lovely ones, *your silence does not serve you!* In fact, your silence… betrays you! You see, living a JUICY life is not an escape route. JUICY is the spirit that connects with herself and other feminine intelligent women in the middle of the *pain* and *piss-ocity*! Being alone in your own head *without adult supervision* is a learned behavior. *We learned* how to hide because self-preservation is a natural law. *We learned* how to figure it out because some of us don't have an internal reference of *support* or *being covered*. Your living turned-on teaches us how to figure it "in," from the inside out. *We learned* how to suffer in silence because speaking up may cost you something. Our voice is a gateway to pleasure, just as our truth is the key that opens the gate. *We learned* how to cover up, cover over, and cover down because at times we had too. The present moment is a point of power to unlearn what no longer serves to live behind the veil. It may take some time, but be patient with your unfolding.

If you have been operating on the above program and other traumatic ones not mentioned, please be advised that the unlearning cannot be avoided. I say this with *love*. It will show up, again and again and again *until you show up, until you come out* and *until you embrace all* of your JUICES. Your tears are orgasmic. They wet your womb so that other seeds planted by the Holy Spirit can water them. Dr. SuZar says this about, the Holy Spirit in her book *The Great Black Mamma of Creation*, "The source of Christian images of the Dove as the Holy Ghost directly stems from Afrakan cosmology. Christian iconography shows seven rays emanating from the Dove of the Holy Ghost. This image is derived from most ancient manifestation of The Great Goddess." While this historical reference enlightened me, I know through my metaphysical studies that the Holy Spirit represents the feminine energy or the Divine Feminine energy. Imagine reading a few verses of your holy text with this in mind. Let your waters flow from your eyes, your womb, and words. You know how I know? Because I was activated by my own juicy journey by chasing orgasm only to find orgasm in me. Pleasure removed the barrier between God and me, even more than I had met with my intellect. I took the risk to live my vision that I would have never taken had I not questioned the vision that didn't come to pass, yet. I am Mother. The Juicy Journey released me from the need of confirmation of my womanhood. I have committed to the Juicy Journey and I have Juicy friends in high places. Look around you and knock, knock… Who's there?

Here are a few ways to stay in your juicy stream. Don't be surprised if the meaning translates into other areas of your life, it's okay because The Juicy Woman is atoned with her life as circle not a box.

1) See yourself as FRUIT, a juicy fruit. And just like it's a challenge to find a succulent peach, it's rare to find women bathing in their own succulent juices. I tend to move fast or so I've told myself. That has caused me to misinterpret many divine messages and moments that were synchronized for my liberation. Therefore, I found myself processing in "hindsight." However, the more I studied my own turn on through pleasure and sensuality, it ministered the message

of slowing down. Picture this sensual scene: One way to *turn up* our succulence is to slooooooow down, feed bite sized pieces to you or your lover's mouth, let the juices spill on their lips, crush the meaty fruit into their stick and lick it off, nibble, bite and do it sloooooooow, while oozing out sounds of pleasure. We can do this with mango or any fruit really. Remember to look into your lover's eyes. Stay with a wordless communication and allow them to feel your worship. Feel me?

2) After we slow down and turn on, create alignment within your body. The body feeds the mind and the mind feeds the spirit. This is the original trinity. So many of the foods that we eat serve to dull our senses and handicap our capacity to question, to be curious, and to create. Dead and poisonous food sources feed our guilt, shame, restrict and add stress, leading to a normal we accepted as being thing like, "it runs in the family." No! It's not true. You are *source energy* in the physical flesh. The resistance to the body and all of its functions as Divine is condemnation of life. Therefore, we must bless the body not only with the words out of our mouths but what we put in it so that we can become lighter. The lighter body releases the mind to connect beyond the body to transcendent source energy.

3) Have *fun*! There is a science to play therapy and certainly pleasure is no different. With pleasure, you exaggerate the focus on the five senses. Simple as that! Have fun with it. All adults have an inner child that either is acting out and

creating havoc because we've undisciplined her or ignored her needs all together. Sometimes the inner child is wounded and those wounds can be attended to, while not taking yourself so seriously. Sometimes, our entire lives become shaped around the wound. I know this firsthand through being joyful, silly, and playful, with a willingness to try new adventures regularly. Let the adventure be with self or others, flirtatiously, if available. Flirting with nature and your food is fun. It tastes better; so, do you. We spend so many years saying no to ourselves because we've heard no many times as children. This journey is to "know" and the only way to do that is to say YES to play and fun, by any means necessary. *Dance*. Especially if you have been heavy laden and yoked by "anything" - GET UP and MOVE, shake, gyrate, twerk, wine, jump, roll, fail, then watch your juices flow again and lead you to that place of revelation.

4) Learn how to ask for help. This is a big one for women who make everyone else a priority or have become invested independent. Independence is truly an illusion. Illusion is a nice way to say, it is a lie. One way to ask for help is in the form of a "request." This is a skill that I teach women right away who say they want this or that but they don't have the resource. Oftentimes, the resource that blocks us from inquiring about possibility is time or money. Time and money are conversations of value. We don't have enough value very often. How I know this is true is because when I look at the things that I've really wanted or wanted to happen, I did whatever it took to make room in my life for it. Asking requires humility and the truth is, so many of us have become so arrogant

about how things look on the outside that we ignore our internal urges, desires and cravings. Begin *within*! Start where you are! Asking for support is a tool of vulnerability through a question or inquiry and being responsive is a signal to the Divine Feminine that you are willing to receive. We have been silent for too long on the areas that matter and cried out on those that don't. Come out! Come out! WHEREVER YOU ARE… dear, Sister!

5) Lean into your Orgasm. It is often shocking to hear from women who have multiple child births and *not one* has had an orgasm or enjoyed sex. In fact, it's far too common. However, one's relationship with orgasm offers more information about the stories and core beliefs that show you in other areas of our intimacy. Intimacy with self deepens intimacy shared with another. Orgasmic living is the ability to move from momentary sensation to extended pleasure that spills into other areas of our lives. Lean in. Go deeper. Spread wider. Let go.

Chapter 9 : The Integrated Woman

A JUICY Spirit is a Goddess in motion towards a pleasure-purpose-passion driven life and is committed to awakening her feminine intelligence, such that she could add to this definition because she has the courage to define herself.

"A goddess is a woman who emerges from deep within herself. She is a woman who has honestly explored her darkness and learned to celebrate her light. She is a woman who is able to fall in love with the magnificent possibilities within her.
She is a woman who knows of the magic and mysterious places inside her, the sacred places that can nurture her soul and make her whole. She is a woman who radiates light. She is magnetic. She walks into a room and male and female alike feel her presence. She has power and softness at the same time. She has powerful sexual energy that's not dependent on physical looks. She has a body that she adores and it shows by the way she comfortably lives and moves in it. She cherishes beauty, light and love. She is a mother to all children. She flows with life in effortless grace. She can heal with a look or a touch of the hand. She is fiercely sensual and fearlessly erotic and engages in sex as

her way to share with another in touching the divine. She is compassion and wisdom. She is seeker of Truth and cares deeply about something bigger than herself. She is a woman who knows that her purpose in life is to reach higher and rule with love. She is woman in love with love. She knows that joy is her destiny and by embracing it and sharing it with others, wounds are healed. She is a woman who has come to know that her partner is as tender, lost, and frightened as she has been at times. She has come to understand the scars of the boy in him and knows that together, love can be the relief, the healing of their wounds. She is a woman who can accept herself as she is. She can accept another as they are. She is able to forgive her mistakes and not feel threatened by another's even when attacked. She is a woman who can ask for help when she needs it or give help when asked. She respects boundaries, hers and another's. She can see God in another's eyes. She can see God in her own. She can see God in every life situation. She is woman who takes responsibility for everything she creates in her life. She is a woman who is totally supportive and giving. She is a Goddess." —Vikram V.

What would you add to the above quote to define Goddess for yourself? First you must become aware of where you may be operating on outdated feminine software. Usually, your unmet desires are the catalyst to get our attention, but we don't have to stay there. Learning to have what we want requires knowing if we want what we have or we are operating on autopilot. Pleasure opens this conversation with the self. Let me share something with you from my heart.

I've known my passion for teaching women a very long time. I get excited about those who come to their process so thirsty. Here's a little intuitive coaching secret: I observe how every woman enters into her process as an indicator of how she will move through it. For some, as soon as "they" say "yes," their actions said "no." I encourage, have individual conversations, and incentivized their participation. Yet, as an empath, I can feel when an individual or a group is moving or not. This process is not for the weak at heart or a woman who has not done her own work. After other sessions I know the difference because, I am often *energized* and *hyped*. When I'm drained and depleted, I know that I'm doing too much of "their" work. I could be over-nurturing. (That's a hint for women who give too much.) That's an indicator for us anywhere that we show up to love, lead, learn or lean.

Given my personal story, I realize that I am one who took my "road less traveled with thirst." I have been blessed to meet Master Trainers along the way. I am the one I speak about who gave my power away with religion, dogma, and performance. I do this work with passion and so much love and *awe* of the majesty that each woman brings. **What I know for sure is, NOTHING JUST HAPPENS!** I have had clients change their mind after agreeing to play fully for their very life force, then begin to only see limitations. I faced it when I had to make a leadership decision about allowing them to remain in this group or in my life. I thought "love" would support transformation and commitment. I had the savior complex. Upon realizing and owning this, I confessed it, and then I surrendered. Now, my point is, even as the coach, I am not exempt from checking in on how I am attracting certain experiences in my life. Oftentimes, leadership positions cause us to hide and cover up the inner journey because we've been trained to do business in a very rigid pretense that only leads to more tension and sometimes victim consciousness. *Nothing* just happens to or around us. Universal Laws are active whether we know what they are entail or not.

One night, I sat on the side of the road for an hour and a half after running out of gas. I couldn't save myself that night. I was moving too fast. I ran out not because I didn't have the money but I thought I would remember on departure. I had jammed packed my schedule and relied upon my crowded mind to remind me. It was the first time this *ever* happened to me. I've played it close before but never had it actually happen. I knew this was a message moment. Remember, *nothing just happens*. I sat wondering, "Who will I call?" I have a so many loved ones that I call friends however, in the moments that matter, I tend to screen their availability before I send forward my ask. Maybe you can relate to having busy-body, purpose-driven friends too. So, I called someone, who I'd really did *not* want to call but he was nearby and it was the quickest way to get off of the overpass. He was willing with less urgency than I desired. I wasn't surprised. On the other hand, my sister friend who invited me out responded, immediately. I realized that night to be more dedicated to my own JUICY. Being out of gas, ain't JUICY but being in a spot of feeling alone and drained isn't either. Oh, *not only that!* My phone died twice. So, I couldn't even call anyone until it recharged. Maybe you can relate? I knew that I have tolerated to the intolerable in order to "be nice." Those twins "be nice" and "be good" are sneaky. You have to watch them because they will talk you out of holding the high road of pleasure.

Be you! Be real! Be Juicy. Integration will require your YES to stretch your boundaries and challenge your limits. The yes journey calls us to go where no woman has gone before at times.

For Example: Only you will I know that a new choice is necessary to interrupt certain patterns that keep you stuck. Your yes won't make sense but it will open your senses. You have to keep stroking in the waters. This is the Juicy, pleasurable journey even when you are first learning how to swim in your own waters. You answer the call on your life more than once. Many people stop when they say yes and never go beyond their answer to the first call. The Divine in you is always calling you forward to answer a higher call that has nothing to do with your conformity and obligations.

JUICY JOURNAL FREEDOM:

How will you integrate your Juicy into your life?

Name seven new choices you are making to lead with pleasure.

Create your own definition of how you will integrate your sensual and your sacred, as an affirmation.

Closing

Pleasure is not a cure all to women's issue. Womanhood is certainly under attack. We all have a role to play in the collective. A part of honoring one another's Juicy Spirit is to know your lane. Your Juicy YES will call you to explore other lanes, but keep it moving. Just like energy you want it to flow. Neither Pleasure, nor Sensual Transformation offers a one size fits all approach. Every woman has the right to explore and push past boxes (core beliefs) that have become too small for her. Know this: You can hit a joy limit. It's a part of the juicy journey too. Pay attention. Usually, nothing is wrong but something doesn't feel right, either. Being FULL on joy can be just as overwhelming as being full on sadness. There *will be* times when you simply must *expand your container and your context* for *joy*, orgasm and bliss. Generational patterns are being recreated by you – *every time you* actively CHOOSE to say YES to what gets your juices flowing! Rather than create drama or wait for it, know you are worthy to be present, supported and gently pushed to even more joy. Joy limits happen when we are growing, expanding, and deepening our relationship with pleasure and being pleasurable.

Have you ever heard the term, "She's feeling herself?" Next time you hear it, give that Goddess a standing ovation. It's a wonderful, delicious and delightful thing to *feel yourself!* My girlfriend spent $90 on pheromone sprays while I just worked my juicy "tools." If you haven't noticed by now, I have been elusive about what all of the tools are, intentionally. Give yourself the experience. It translates better, when you get it how you live. I can tell you that I have witnessed myself as a walking *pheromone* at times! I am a magnet to my desires and sometimes I have to blush when they sneak up on me. The sensual awakening encourages a woman to feel herself. The option to not feeling yourself is to be numb. The sacred yes extends the juicy journey and allows you to give yourself permission to feel your way toward your good, trusting it is the surrender that is required. Give yourself the experience.

Surrender is not easy all the time for women who don't know or don't trust not knowing. I understand. We all acquire experiences along our life path that armor us, and that armor looks like achievement at times and resignation at others. With surrender comes the art of receiving. This is very important for expanding orgasm. Even if we have great orgasms, there is more available in the body beyond the clitoris. We are capable of having chakra orgasms and even astral orgasms with committed practice and a lifestyle that aligns with deliberately moving the energy. Yin energy is not limited to gender, however it's no secret that many women struggle with receiving, although we long for it. So many of us just want to let go and having someone hold our hand, while knowing that we are safe. I know I did. As a strong Amazon woman, this skill of surrender was not automatic with me. However, this submission below is what juicy opens your sacred power to shift anything:

Our sister reframed one of the most sensitive wounds that the yoni holds onto. She not only shared this once but gave me permission to share it far and wide. Our YES takes the poison out of wounds, even after we've been stung. This Juicy Goddess did this with so much eloquence:

"I have noticed over the years the huge number of women that have been raped, molested or abused. The numbers are staggering. I am also in that number. At the age of 16 (I was a virgin), I was "raped" and ridiculed. For it to be my first experience, I was hurt, humiliated, and steeped in grief for my virginity. I became what I called THEN "damaged goods." I slept with many many men. I was affiliated with a very tough gang. I was around shootings, drugs, and many illegal activities. I had more then 30 friends killed. I had several abortions and a miscarriage. I blamed my missing mother for everything. My sister literally saved my life numerous times. After alllllll of that, one day I woke up and I found my power back. I became the victor instead of the victim. I changed MY story! Now when I speak of the "rape," I send love to him. He NEEDED my healing pussy. I healed him! All of the men I slept with I HEALED them. I AM that powerful. If you have the pleasure of entering my sacred place, you are blessed for life. This is not me being arrogant but standing in my power. I stand TODAY a warrior and I made it through! Thank you, GOD! I'm having a moment right now Sistahs so bear with me as I shed these tears of my journey! I kept looking for a GOD in the sky to save me! I was a Muslim, Christian, Catholic, and even practiced Buddhism and Tantra looking for GOD. It wasn't

until I realized what I was looking for I WAS. All I had to do was look in the mirror. My entire life I created, so I needed to put my director's cap back on and get to work. I fired the actors in my life that were no longer needed. I hired new actors that resonated with who I was waking up to be. With my Angels, Spirit Guides, and Ancestors backing me I knew I could overcome any storm. It doesn't matter if you were molested, raped, had abortions, etc. You are whole and complete TODAY. Working with La Tonia will help you remember who you really are. It's a new day, Ladies. All is well." —**R. C.**

I didn't have to coach this because she became her own Inner Guru. This can happen for any woman that turns her own water into wine. You are the living miracle. This is the miraculous rites of passage for the woman who chooses to take on the most traumatic conversation and reframe it for her good and the good of those who love her. Needless to say, this sharing inspired others in our Juicy circle. The following response was just as inspiring from one our physicians in the circle.

"Molestation, rape, trauma, makes us either go OUTside of ourselves (what some call HYPERsexualism in medicine) or it makes you go INSide ourselves (HYPOSEXUAL). That's what all that trauma did for me. It made me RIGID and COLD like a GLACIER and then the place that should have provided a source of feminine healing for me – Christianity rewarded me for being

sexually RIGID! That's the same hot ass mess in reverse! (Remember I said I was fondled and almost raped but I still felt the shame of the incidents). It's just more acceptable because it keeps up with whatever facade "religion" is trying to uphold. Then I became SHAMED about being not just a virgin but an old ass virgin who no less was being paid BIG money to talk to people all over the globe about their "sexual dysfunctions" however they presented themselves. NEVER from a place of judgement because I see myself in those around me but what I could see even more clearly is that I HAD THE SAME SEXUAL DYSFUNCTIONS. Hear my heart. It wasn't until recent years, maybe the past FIVE that I realized all those people TRYING to put me on a pedestal to ENDORSE their cause is what FUELED my fire to GET the hell outta there and I mean FAST! Because although they were putting ME up to be a spokesperson, they were WORSE than the patients I cared for. Not worse because they were sexual BUT worse for hypocritically condemning folks for doing the exact same things THEY were doing. Please believe I have no malice in my heart because I got out from the matrix. I'm just sharing with great passion! Y'all some bad chicas! Who else would allow us to be this open without judgement? Again, I say, it was well! It is well and it's goin' be well! I receive that for my life and everyone connected to me... Thank you for allowing me to share this!"

"What the caterpillar calls the end of the world, the master calls a butterfly."
⊠**Bach**

You are worthy to live through conscious choice and be co-creative with the essence of yourself, which is God/Goddess/Holy I AM/Force/Power/JUICE! One way to access that is to make a choice and entertain (host) your Divinity Truth and Forgiveness. Shame and Guilt are terrible twins that have clones imbedded in mores of this culture. Question them! Do your own investigation of the truth and know that the answer lives in the same room as the question. You are the answer that you've been waiting for to be your own JUICY GOOD THING!

Juicy Q & A

Let's end with practical ways to integrate a few JUICY principles that show up in the lives of women I have coached. Sometimes after all of this spiritual talk, it sounds a lot like fluff. The juicy waters flow deep and you'll get to read questions from my clients who jumped in at their level. My answers may support similar questions that you may have or didn't know you had. Send your questions to my website: LaToniaTaylor.com or to the same on all social media platforms.

ONE

Question: How do you determine if you're a good lover? I've heard several butterflies say (in so many words), that they are good/great/capable lovers. I honestly don't know how to determine if I'm a good lover. I've been told that I am a good lover, but compared to what? Any and all input is appreciated.

Answer: Great question! What do you enjoy? List it! Think of your "greatest" lovers and your worst ones. What did they do? When you determine that, reflect on: Do you give that? Do you participate or initiate? Do you flirt? Even if you are in a relationship you should do so. Unfortunately, people often stop flirting. Play is important. Physical play is even better. Finally, once you think about it, give yourself permission to experiment! It's not a head game.

TWO

Question: I've experienced lower back pain and pelvic pain on a regular basis. I believe that the pain I am experiencing are my hurts, anxieties, insecurities, and distrust. I also believe this is why I have not experienced an orgasm in past relationships. I have always been afraid to be vulnerable, and therefore never allowed myself to give into my emotions. I am beginning the process of healing, but I am noticing the layers and the depth of my pain.

Answer: Great job, listening to your body. Celebrate the noticing. Remember what you focus on grows. The intention is to MOVE it. The acknowledgment of pain is purposeful. I applaud your strong work! I see you coming alive. I would say continue the work by getting touched in those places where you have noticed pain. You can do this by having a massage or a reiki session.

THREE

Question: So, in honor of myself and Clitoris Awareness Week, I want to reconnect with my pussy. No toys today! Just us reconnecting and remembering those pleasure spots. Any thoughts…

Answer: This is SO DIVINE! So JUICY! I encourage you to spend time with your yoni in a non-sexual way as well. In fact, have you gotten a yoni egg yet? If so, create a space with a candle, and speak prayers or affirmations into the egg. While touching and talking to your yoni, ASK HER for permission to enter. Check to see if she is ready (lubricated) enough to receive the egg and then slowly insert (NOT PUSH) the egg, such that she can suck the egg in the rest of the way. Honing and holding the arousal is how we bring our turn on into our world. Just like you have already.

FOUR

Question: Why is it important to ask your yoni for permission to enter? Should you do this whenever you are in a moment of pleasure? How do you dismiss the fear of pain? I bought my first toy, which was really hard to do, because I'm still dispelling the myth that pleasure/masturbation is wrong and a sin. I attempted to use my toy but became utterly afraid to use/insert it for fear of it hurting. I've always felt tense, tight or whatever you call it in my private area or my (p).

Answer: I'd like to engage you from your heart, which is connected to your yoni, instead of your head. There are answers in both your head and your heart that will override my feedback. I offer you *to surrender to doing it wrong*. YOU, as GODDESS, are a *living laboratory* that you are exploring! That said, specifically for the egg work (play) what comes to you as the reason for "asking for permission?"

It's really a way to explore and, it's a way to develop relationship. You are not literally "asking a question." You are asking with the intent of connecting your body and your spirit. You see? The atonement. No separation. You are listening with the signals your yoni gives and yes, lubrication is one, sensation is another, and simply a YES in your spirit is a big one. Now, all of this could be called *reverence*. When you practice *reverence*, you attract the same.

FIVE

Question: My marriage seems more like a business arrangement these days… where my husband and I are like two ships passing in the night. From the outside it looks perfect… 3200 sq. ft home, luxury cars in the garage, a man that is a super father to his children, and takes care of all the bills. So why am I unhappy? Why am I experiencing unfulfilled intimacy, with a fear that my battery is dying? Why am I feeling a loss of interest for pleasure, and more importantly a loss of interest in pleasure with my "life partner?" I have to ask myself, am I willing to do a different thing to achieve the desire of complete fulfillment? Am I willing to sacrifice a comfortable lifestyle for the pursuit of pleasure? And do I really have to?

Answer: Congratulations! You just opened a *vortex* for yourself to co-create with the Divinity that you are. You just defied one strong hold and what does your coach say? KEEP GOING! First, your pleasure begins with knowing what you desire. If that is sex with your husband, then that sounds like an easy fix, right? Maybe not. However, it would be worth fighting for, playing with, and tuning up if so.

If it's something else still not expressed… something that you are pretending not to know or to be… then that's another matter. Secondly, women who give advice to other women from their own quiet desperation ends *today*! It matters not whether an awakened woman is single or married to be able to stand for another sister's truth. Intimacy is into-me-I-see. Before you make any decisions to do your *own investigation* of your truth, *begin within*! Communication is the heartbeat of any relationship however; it begins with the relationship with ourselves.

I offer you that this process is intended to elevate pleasure, not minimize it. How do you define pleasure? How each woman defines her pursuit of pleasure begins with the first step towards IT, whatever her IT is. No woman is to judge that unless she is causing harm to herself or another woman, consciously.

You have not felt or done anything that another woman has not done or felt and not just survived, but thrived. I am one of them. I left a beautiful home, with a man who paid all of the bills (except a few), and was adored by some or seemed harmless to many, even my own mother. I had to remember my mother's message to me growing up, "Sometimes, a piece of man is better than *no man* at all and if he comes home every night and goes to work, you'll be fine." That was her reality. I was not supported at first. I moved anyway. I faced the shadows of my *ego* that had lied to me leading me to end up in this place. You see, this was my second husband. It was being in a community of women that I began to ask the questions I was initially embarrassed to speak. Then I immersed myself in the play and pleasure. The answers began to unfold through raising the vibration just a little, then a little more until I was processed by pleasure (loving and nurturing myself and my desires). I awakened. I was supported. My womanhood was spared years of self-deceit. And, I also offer you that all relationships can "work."

SIX

Question: What do I do about my sexless marriage? Shouldn't he just know what I need after all these years?

Answer: I often tell my clients and those around me, "Don't let anyone SHOULD on you!" Why would you expect that he "should" know? Have you used your throat chakra, elevated your *turn on* in yourself, *flirted* with him, made dates, and space for him? Lowered your shirt line and raised your skirt? Do you wear skirts? Do you practice seduction when you walk past him in the house? Use your seductive power when you look at him? And most of all… have you asked him how he wants to be teased and pleased? So, SEXLESS is a symptom my love. The Sensual Awakened Woman gets to the root (no pun intended). First, you get to your own root programs about yourself and your sex. Make new choices. Grieve the old ones. Then, from a cooler place (with no heat), go to him and make requests. *Know* you have *not done anything wrong*!

SEVEN

Question: I spent many lonely days in my room crying as a little girl. I was not planned and everyone in my family reminds me that I was a mistake or accident. Where do I begin the forgiveness process in order to find my juicy self-love again?

Answer: This is another area where many sisters are not alone and think that they are. The silence, isolation, contempt, and indifference you both (parents and child) experienced does not define you. That's really important to take in. Even for your parents; it was more of a reflection of their ability or capacity and the lack there-of. Once you begin moving this energy, it will be important to layer it for repetitive acts of forgiveness. Forgiveness, first of any decisions, choices and beliefs that you've held about yourself along the way. *Forgiveness is the universal cleanser*... but... not before you are ready. Some of us, who have withheld and held in, need to give ourselves permission to *get righteously mad* and sit in the feeling before trying to fix and answer the why nots. That becomes your knot. You are in your flow sister and beautiful for the asking. You are Divine! Your anointing is no less special for feeling and speaking your truth, *as it is!* Now, what do you declare for yourself? What are your new definitions? How does it look? Feel? Smell? Taste? Sound? Ummm hmmmm… you know! Your soul knows.

EIGHT

Question: Is there ever a time when those who have made the Juicy Spirit journey feel "not-so-juicy?" I guess what I am searching for is the "knowingness." For instance, I can live in the pleasure zone, then wake up one morning, and just not feel it, and from there, it is a challenge to find my place again. Do I need meds? (smile)

Answer: Pleasure requires discipline, my love. Real simple, not real deep. "Repetition is the mother of skill." Your meds are your own juices. "What tools can I use that my juicy coaching process has seeded in to my life?" or "What do I need to get JUICY or get my JUICES flowing?" Some may call it research; I call it *exploration*! So, for instance, you will never really know what lights your fire if you don't become curious, in your own unique way. If it serves you, add it to your tool box and if it doesn't keep it moving. Then, there are those times when what's going on is a signal to *sit in the lotus*. So, the answers vary!

On the flip side, who told you your "darkness" (irritability, annoyance, etc.) is not juicy? I've accepted my dark side and I'm just as juicy and fierce in them, as my bright days. You are never *not* juicy. You just have, not Juicy moments. It's your programming that needs changing.

NINE

Question: I have been paying more attention to myself and my yoni. I notice that she is becoming more moist. Is this normal?

Answer: Yes, very normal. When we deliberately focus on anything… that "thing" grows or expands. For example, when I decided that I was going to own a brand-new red Jaguar, the more I focused on that intention, the more I began to see that car everywhere! Have you ever thought about someone you haven't spoken to in a long while and all of a sudden you see them at the supermarket or they just happen to call to say "Hi"? You created it! Our thoughts create our reality. So, focusing on your yoni and giving her the attention she deserves, allows her to communicate with you in the form of being moist. You should *always* be wet. I've noticed that when I'm stressed, tired, or irritable I don't have one drop of wetness! I'm not in my pleasure! When I'm in my pleasure and connected to my femininity, I am always wet.

TEN

Question: I'm a mature woman who experienced the inconsistency of my lover, soulmate actually. He left and I doubted myself. For a moment, I questioned myself deeply. But more importantly, his leaving caused me to question my sex appeal and I began to buy into the belief that aging (60+) had diminished my sexual desire and appeal. My emphasis has shifted to what pleases me and now that my senses are being awakened I see, feel, touch,

taste, smell, listen, and love in new ways. My zest for life is the highest ever and I am the best I've ever been. And that partner who walked away, well he asked if he could come back and I said yes. Am I juicy or what?

Answer: You are seasoned and juicy! That said, did you have an opportunity to explore two things: 1) Reason for infrequency; and, 2) What *new* agreements you and your partner have? I salute your courage to *go for the yes*, rather than play a game of victim. That's courageous. In addition, I offer that mates are mirrors. What did his leaving mirror? What did his return mirror? This is an opportunity to renegotiate inside and out. *That's good stuff!* Thank you for illustrating how it can happen for *anyone*! I certainly can relate. I am an amazingly sexual woman however, I desire the tenderness and devotion that make my juices come alive. Even sporadic lovers, just won't do. I have a new agreement with myself and the key word is: Investment! Women need to understand that doesn't always equal marriage. In other words, sometimes we get to enjoy our juicy exploration without putting a price on it. You are priceless beyond contracts because the first and only contract that is sacred is the one you make and live with yourself FIRST.

ELEVEN

Question: I'm feeling MOTHY! I bumped into an old man-friend and his wife. This was the one with whom I had planned on building a wonderful life with and having children. His family and mother *loved* me, and my family was digging him. Anyway, we went our separate ways a long while ago but I

couldn't help but look at his wife and begin to do the *very* thing I tell ladies not to do: COMPARE myself to her! Is she nicer? Are her kisses sweeter? Is her honey smoother? Maybe her jokes are funnier. Does he feel safer with her? Maybe they share the same history...

Answer: You all are so beautiful in the Lotus!! Moving energy with intention is what I see. Did you consider how powerful your pussy is to call *that* man forth to stir your desire pot? Ummm Hmmm! Rather than tell yourself to "get over it," the Goddess surfs the waves of emotion. Why? It holds messages for you. When you are powerful and present, you can ride it out. It then allows you to release residual *unexpressed grief* and disappointment. Surfing the wave of the painful allows you to surf the waves of orgasm. I offer this: fine china is strong, it just has to be handled with care.

About The Author

Sometimes it's the patterns in your life that tell your story. I realized that my professional and creative commitments had a common theme: Vision, Strategy, Activation, Emergence via Spiritual Psychology.

La Tonia Taylor has cultivated her life experience, community service, professional training, and faith walks into a spiritual testimony. Born and raised in the deep South, La Tonia is naturally inspirational! La Tonia's has her own testimony, tests, and triumph that required her to demonstrate her own rebirth. Now, a Purpose, Pleasure Passion Counselor, Healing Educator, and Spiritual Mid-Wife, who leads others to her signature blend of Spiritual Psychology, Transformation and Feminine Soul Retrieval Rites of Passage programs. She is also a Coach and Production Consultant on Emmy Award Winning Show on The OWN Network with her mentor, Rev. Dr. Iyanla Vanzant's - **Iyanla, Fix My Life**.

Her Message: ReBirth & Emerge Transformed.

Her programs share how "ReBirth and ReInvention is NOT a one-time event!" Therefore, these audiences have extended to sectors in community, corporations, and organizations redesigning and implementing new program goals, in order to accomplish their overall mission statement and strategy. In the Corporate sector, La Tonia is a Specialist in Program Organizational Development and provided training in areas such as; Conflict Resolution, Restorative Justice, and

Employment/Career Preparation.

Beginning at Southern University in Baton Rouge to focus on Elementary Education, her student journey led to Mastery of the inner journey. La Tonia holds a Bachelor of Arts in Psychology and Human Development from Union Institute and University; she is also an Inaugural Graduate of The Inner Visions Institute for Spiritual Development, also founded Dr. Vanzant and is now a Master-level Trained Life Coach and an Ordained Minister. With Certifications in various Healing arts; such as Reiki, Iridology, Tantric Massage, Goddess Rites and Holistic Nutrition.

This Multi-Passionate soul has served as Faculty at The Inner Visions Institute for Spiritual Development, Associate Minister at Union Temple Baptist Church and Board Member/Minister at Real Life Today Church. Thus, in The Market-place, she is affectionately known as; The RevCoach. With celebrity clients and women worldwide, Author La Tonia is a Spiritual Midwife of Purpose, Pleasure & Passion Suite of Programs, Services, and Spiritual Community.

Juicy Programs

Level I: Good Girls Gone Goddess ~ An open source virtual community to cultivate the feminine arts with a diverse tribe of women from all walks of life on Facebook, where women are GROWING FORTH beyond "others" expectations, (hidden or in plain sight) that have locked, suppressed or sabotaged our relationship with Love, Sex & Money.

Level II: The Juicy YOU ~ 30 Days Living in Your Sweet Spot ~ A 30 Day Program where you will ACTIVATE your feminine thirst for sweetness and satisfaction in your Love, Sex and Money life and succulence that will fill your cup with radical juicy self-care activities so that you spill over into any area of your life or long-held desires. The process designed to experience immersion and inclusion in a gentle way rather than more sacrifice to access information that you may already have within you.

Level III: The Juicy "Spirit" Womanhood -Rites of Passage ~ A 6 month Rites of Passage Program for Adult Women designed to rebirth Purpose, Pleasure and Passion in a experiential "feminine soul retrieval" process via the art of sensual transformation tools to manifest a woman's vision for her life, business and legacy.

- 6 Modules loaded with supportive activities to experiment and explore week to week.
- A RICH immersion experience in a deeply supported Mastermind
- Areas of Focus: Foundations, Creativity/Orgasm, Money/ Abundance, Expression/Identity, Courage/Forgiveness, Communication with self/others, Communication with The Divine and Spiritual Gifts
- Self-Paced
- Group Coaching and unlimited Individual Support
- Special Guest Supplemental
- A Special Consecration Ceremony and retreat weekend to seal the gateways opened each month.
- Special Alumni Access to advanced supplemental

Next Level: Private VIP Retreats ~ Customized 1:1 support in a luxury setting for busy clients who require high value and limited time. Learn more on the website.

Note: Private Coaching & Booking is Accessible All Year

www.ingramcontent.com/pod-product-compliance
Lightning Source LLC
Chambersburg PA
CBHW051410070526
44584CB00023B/3373